PRENTICE HALL

MAGRUDER'S

AMERICAN GOVERNMENT

Guided Reading and Review Workbook

D1567210

PEARSON
Prentice Hall

Weeks-Townsend Memorial Library
Union College
Barbourville, KY 40906

Needham, Massachusetts
Upper Saddle River, New Jersey
Glenview, Illinois

PEARSON
Prentice
Hall

ISBN 0-13-067955-0

15 16 17 18   09 08 07 06

BD

TABLE OF CONTENTS

Success in social studies comes from doing three things well—reading, testing, and writing. The following pages present strategies to help you read for meaning, understand test questions, and write well.

Reading for Meaning

Do you have trouble remembering what you read? Here are some tips from experts that will improve your ability to recall and understand what you read:

BEFORE YOU READ

Preview the text to identify important information.
Like watching the coming attractions at a movie theater, previewing the text helps you know what to expect. Study the questions and strategies below to learn how to preview what you read.

Ask yourself these questions:	Use these strategies to find the answers:
• What is the text about?	Read the headings, subheadings, and captions. Study the photos, maps, tables, or graphs.
• What do I already know about the topic?	Read the questions at the end of the text to see if you can answer any of them.
• What is the purpose of the text?	Turn the headings into *who, what, when, where, why,* or *how* questions. This will help you decide if the text compares things, tells a chain of events, or explains causes and effects.

Organize information in a way that helps you see meaningful connections or relationships.

Taking notes as you read will improve your understanding. Use graphic organizers like the ones below to record the information you read. Study these descriptions and examples to learn how to create each type of organizer.

Sequencing

A **flowchart** helps you see how one event led to another. It can also display the steps in a process.

Use a flowchart if the text—
- tells about a chain of events.
- explains a method of doing something.

TIP▶ List the events or steps in order.

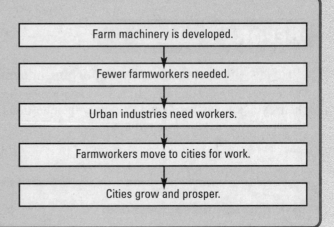

Farm machinery is developed.

Fewer farmworkers needed.

Urban industries need workers.

Farmworkers move to cities for work.

Cities grow and prosper.

Comparing and Contrasting

A **Venn diagram** displays similarities and differences.

Use a Venn diagram if the text—
- compares and contrasts two individuals, groups, places, things, or events.

TIP▶ Label the outside section of each circle and list differences.
Label the shared section and list similarities.

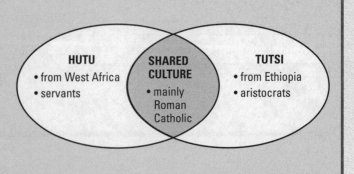

HUTU
- from West Africa
- servants

SHARED CULTURE
- mainly Roman Catholic

TUTSI
- from Ethiopia
- aristocrats

AS YOU READ

(continued)

Categorizing Information

A **chart** organizes information in categories.

Use a chart if the text—
- lists similar facts about several places or things.
- presents characteristics of different groups.

TIP▶ Write an appropriate heading for each column in the chart to identify its category.

COUNTRY	FORM OF GOVERNMENT	ECONOMY
Cuba	communist dictatorship	command economy
Puerto Rico	democracy	free enterprise system

Identifying Main Ideas and Details

A **concept web** helps you understand relationships among ideas.

Use a concept web if the text—
- provides examples to support a main idea.
- links several ideas to a main topic.

TIP▶ Write the main idea in the largest circle. Write details in smaller circles and draw lines to show relationships.

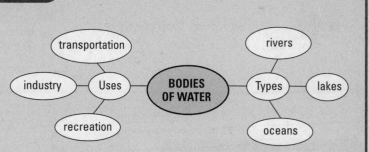

Organizing Information

An **outline** provides an overview, or a kind of blueprint for reading.

Use an outline to organize ideas—
• according to their importance.
• according to the order in which they are presented.

TIP▶ Use Roman numerals for main ideas, capital letters for secondary ideas, and Arabic numerals for supporting details.

> **I. Differences Between the North and the South**
>   **A.** Views on slavery
>   **1.** Northern abolitionists
>   **2.** Southern slave owners
>   **B.** Economies
>   **1.** Northern manufacturing
>   **2.** Southern agriculture

Identifying Cause and Effect

A **cause-and-effect** diagram shows the relationship between what happened (effect) and the reason why it happened (cause).

Use a cause-and-effect chart if the text—
• lists one or more causes for an event.
• lists one or more results of an event.

TIP▶ Label causes and effects. Draw arrows to indicate how ideas are related.

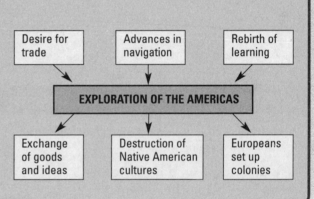

AFTER YOU READ

Test yourself to find out what you learned from reading the text.

Go back to the questions you asked yourself before you read the text. You should be able to give more complete answers to these questions:
• What is the text about?
• What is the purpose of the text?

You should also be able to make connections between the new information you learned from the text and what you already knew about the topic.

Study your graphic organizer. Use this information as the *answers*. Make up a meaningful *question* about each piece of information.

Taking Tests

Do you panic at the thought of taking a standardized test? Here are some tips that most test developers recommend to help you achieve good scores.

MULTIPLE-CHOICE QUESTIONS

Read each part of a multiple-choice question to make sure you understand what is being asked.

Many tests are made up of multiple-choice questions. Some multiple-choice items are **direct questions.** They are complete sentences followed by possible answers, called distractors.

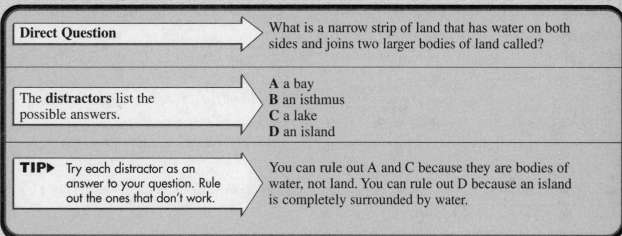

Direct Question → What is a narrow strip of land that has water on both sides and joins two larger bodies of land called?

The **distractors** list the possible answers. →
A a bay
B an isthmus
C a lake
D an island

TIP▶ Try each distractor as an answer to your question. Rule out the ones that don't work. → You can rule out A and C because they are bodies of water, not land. You can rule out D because an island is completely surrounded by water.

Other multiple-choice questions are **incomplete sentences** that you are to finish. They are followed by possible answers.

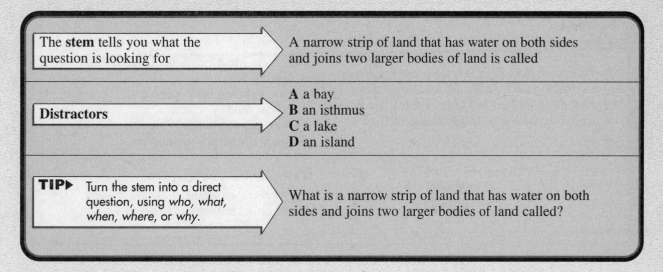

The **stem** tells you what the question is looking for → A narrow strip of land that has water on both sides and joins two larger bodies of land is called

Distractors →
A a bay
B an isthmus
C a lake
D an island

TIP▶ Turn the stem into a direct question, using *who, what, when, where,* or *why.* → What is a narrow strip of land that has water on both sides and joins two larger bodies of land called?

WHAT'S BEING TESTED?

Identify the type of question you are being asked.

Social studies tests often ask questions that involve reading comprehension. Other questions may require you to gather or interpret information from a map, graph, or chart. The following strategies will help you answer different kinds of questions.

Reading Comprehension Questions

What to do:

1. Determine the content and organization of the selection.

2. Analyze the questions.
Do they ask you to *recall facts?*

Do they ask you to *make judgments?*

3. Read the selection.

4. Answer the questions.

How to do it:

Read the **title.** Skim the selection. Look for key words that indicate time, cause-and-effect, or comparison.

Look for **key words** in the stem:
<u>According to</u> the selection . . .
The selection <u>states</u> that . . .

The <u>main idea</u> of the selection is . . .
The author <u>would likely</u> agree that . . .

Read quickly. Keep the questions in mind.

Try out each distractor and choose the best answer. Refer back to the selection if necessary.

Example:
A Region of Diversity The Khmer empire was one of many kingdoms in Southeast Asia. Unlike the Khmer empire, however, the other kingdoms were small because Southeast Asia's mountains kept people protected and apart. People had little contact with those who lived outside their own valley.

Why were most kingdoms in Southeast Asia small?
A disease killed many people
B lack of food
C climate was too hot
D mountains kept people apart

TIP▶ The key word <u>because</u> tells why the king-doms were small.
(The correct answer is D.)

Map Questions

What to do:	How to do it:
1. Determine what kind of information is presented on the map.	Read the map **title.** It will indicate the purpose of the map. Study the **map key.** It will explain the symbols used on the map. Look at the **scale.** It will help you calculate distance between places on the map.
2. Read the question. Determine which component on the map will help you find the answer.	Look for **key words** in the stem. About <u>how far</u> . . . [use the scale] <u>What crops</u> were grown in . . . [use the map key]
3. Look at the map and answer the question in your own words.	Do not read the distractors yet.
4. Choose the best answer.	Decide which distractor agrees with the answer you determined from the map.

Eastern Europe: Language Groups

In which of these countries are Thraco-Illyrian languages spoken?

A Romania
B Albania
C Hungary
D Lithuania

TIP▶ Read the labels and the key to understand the map.
(The correct answer is B.)

KEY
- Slavic languages
- Romance languages
- Thraco-Illyrian languages
- Baltic languages
- Non-Indo-European languages

Lambert Azimuthal Equal-Area Projection

Graph Questions

What to do:

1. Determine the purpose of the graph.

2. Determine what information on the graph will help you find the answer.

3. Choose the best answer.

How to do it:

Read the graph **title.** It indicates what the graph represents.

Read the **labels** on the graph or on the key. They tell the units of measurement used by the graph.

Decide which distractor agrees with the answer you determined from the graph.

Example

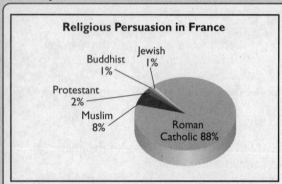

A **Circle graph** shows the relationship of parts to the whole in terms of percentages.

After Roman Catholics, the next largest religious population in France is
A Buddhist   **C** Jewish
B Protestant   **D** Muslim

TIP▶ Compare the percentages listed in the labels.
(The correct answer is D.)

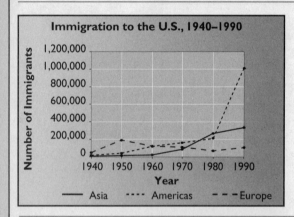

A **line graph** shows a pattern or change over time by the direction of the line.

Between 1980 and 1990, immigration to the U.S. from the Americas
A decreased a little   **C** stayed about the same
B increased greatly   **D** increased a little

TIP▶ Compare the vertical distance between the two
          correct points on the line graph.
(The correct answer is B.)

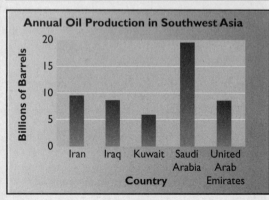

A **bar graph** compares differences in quantity by showing bars of different lengths.

Saudi Arabia produces about how many more billion of barrels of oil a year than Iran?
A 5 million   **C** 15 million
B 10 million   **D** 20 million

TIP▶ Compare the heights of the bars to find the
          difference.
(The correct answer is B.)

Writing for Social Studies

When you face a writing assignment, do you think, "How will I ever get through this?" Here are some tips to guide you through any writing project from start to finish.

THE WRITING PROCESS

Follow each step of the writing process to communicate effectively.

Step 1. Prewrite

- Establish the purpose.
- Define the topic.
- Determine the audience.
- Gather details.

Step 2. Draft

- Organize information logically in an outline or graphic organizer.
- Write an introduction, body, and conclusion.
- State main ideas clearly.
- Include relevant details to support your ideas.

Step 3. Revise

- Edit for clarity of ideas and elaboration.

Step 4. Proofread

- Correct any errors in spelling, grammar, and punctuation.

Step 5. Publish and Present

- Copy text neatly by hand, or use a typewriter or word processor.
- Illustrate as needed.
- Create a cover, if appropriate.

TYPES OF WRITING FOR SOCIAL STUDIES

Identify the purpose for your writing.

Each type of writing assignment has a specific purpose, and each purpose needs a different plan for development. The following descriptions and examples will help you identify the three purposes for social studies writing. The lists of steps will help you plan your writing.

Writing to Inform

Purpose: to present facts or ideas

Example
During the 1960s, research indicated the dangers of the insecticide DDT. It killed insects but also had long-term effects. When birds and fish ate poisoned insects, DDT built up in their fatty tissue. The poison also showed up in human beings who ate birds and fish contaminated by DDT.

TIP▶ Look for these **key terms** in the assignment: explain, describe, report, narrate

How to get started:
- Determine the topic you will write about.
- Write a topic sentence that tells the main idea.
- List all the ideas you can think of that are related to the topic.
- Arrange the ideas in logical order.

Writing to Persuade

Purpose: to influence someone

Example
Teaching computer skills in the classroom uses time that could be spent teaching students how to think for themselves or how to interact with others. Students who can reason well, express themselves clearly, and get along with other people will be better prepared for life than those who can use a computer.

TIP▶ Look for these **key terms** in the assignment: convince, argue, request

How to get started:
- Make sure you understand the problem or issue clearly.
- Determine your position.
- List evidence to support your arguments.
- Predict opposing views.
- List evidence you can use to overcome the opposing arguments.

Writing to Provide Historical Interpretations

Purpose: to present the perspective of someone in a different era

Example
The crossing took a week, but the steamship voyage was hard. We were cramped in steerage with hundreds of others. At last we saw the huge statue of the lady with the torch. In the reception center, my mother held my hand while the doctor examined me. Then, my father showed our papers to the official, and we collected our bags. I was scared as we headed off to find a home in our new country.

TIP▶ Look for these **key terms** in the assignment: go back in time, create, suppose that, if you were

How to get started:
- Study the events or issues of the time period you will write about.
- Consider how these events or issues might have affected different people at the time.
- Choose a person whose views you would like to present.
- Identify the thoughts and feelings this person might have experienced.

RESEARCH FOR WRITING

Follow each step of the writing process to communicate effectively.

After you have identified the purpose for your writing, you may need to do research. The following steps will help you plan, gather, organize, and present information.

Step 1. Ask Questions

| Ask yourself questions to help guide your research. | What do I already know about the topic? What do I want to find out about the topic? |

Step 2. Acquire Information

| Locate and use appropriate sources of information about the topic. | Library Internet search Interviews |
| Take notes. | Follow accepted format for listing sources. |

Step 3. Analyze Information

| Evaluate the information you find. | Is it relevant to the topic? Is it up-to-date? Is it accurate? Is the writer an authority on the topic? Is there any bias? |

Step 4. Use Information

| Answer your research questions with the information you have found. (You may find that you need to do more research.) | Do I have all the information I need? |
| Organize your information into the main points you want to make. Identify supporting details. | Arrange ideas in outline form or in a graphic organizer. |

Step 5. Communicate What You've Learned

Review the purpose for your writing and choose an appropriate way to present the information.

Purpose	Presentation
inform	formal paper, documentary, multimedia
persuade	essay, letter to the editor, speech
interpret	journal, newspaper account, drama

Draft and revise your writing, and then evaluate it. Use a rubric for self-evaluation.

EVALUATING YOUR WRITING

Use the following rubric to help you evaluate your writing.

	Excellent	Good	Acceptable	Unacceptable
Purpose	Achieves purpose—to inform, persuade, or provide historical interpretation—very well	Informs, persuades, or provides historical interpretation reasonably well	Reader cannot easily tell if the purpose is to inform, persuade, or provide historical interpretation	Lacks purpose
Organization	Develops ideas in a very clear and logical way	Presents ideas in a reasonably well-organized way	Reader has difficulty following the organization	Lacks organization
Elaboration	Explains all ideas with facts and details	Explains most ideas with facts and details	Includes some supporting facts and details	Lacks supporting details
Use of Language	Uses excellent vocabulary and sentence structure with no errors in spelling, grammar, or punctuation	Uses good vocabulary and sentence structure with very few errors in spelling, grammar, or punctuation	Includes some errors in grammar, punctuation, and spelling	Includes many errors in grammar, punctuation, and spelling

Section 1: Guided Reading and Review
Government and the State

A. As You Read

As you read Section 1, fill in the answers to the following questions.

1. What are the four characteristics of a state?

    a. _____

    b. _____

    c. _____

    d. _____

2. What are the four theories of the origins of a state?

    a. _____

    b. _____

    c. _____

    d. _____

3. What are six purposes of the American system of government?

    a. _____

    b. _____

    c. _____

    d. _____

    e. _____

    f. _____

B. Reviewing Key Terms

Define the following terms. Write your answers on a separate sheet of paper.

4. government

5. public policy

6. legislative power

7. executive power

8. judicial power

9. constitution

10. dictatorship

11. democracy

12. state

13. sovereign

Section 2: Guided Reading and Review
Forms of Government

A. As You Read

Use the chart below to compare the democratic form of government to the dictatorship form of government.

	Democracy	Dictatorship
Sovereign power is held by:	1.	2.
Those who rule are responsible to:	3.	4.
Power is gained by:	5.	6.

B. Reviewing Key Terms

Match the descriptions in Column I with the terms in Column II. Write the correct letter in each blank.

Column I

_____ 7. a government in which a single person holds unlimited power

_____ 8. a government in which the executive and legislative branches are separate and coequal

_____ 9. a government in which power is divided between a central government and other local governments

_____ 10. a government in which a small, usually self-appointed, group has the power to rule

_____ 11. a government in which all power belongs to a central agency

_____ 12. an alliance of independent states

_____ 13. structuring a government so that power is shared by a central and several local governments

_____ 14. a government in which members of the executive branch are also members of the legislative branch and are subject to the legislature's direct control

Column II

a. unitary government
b. federal government
c. confederation
d. presidential government
e. parliamentary government
f. division of powers
g. oligarchy
h. autocracy

Section 3: Guided Reading and Review
Basic Concepts of Democracy

A. As You Read

On the chart below, write the five basic concepts of democracy and write a sentence describing each.

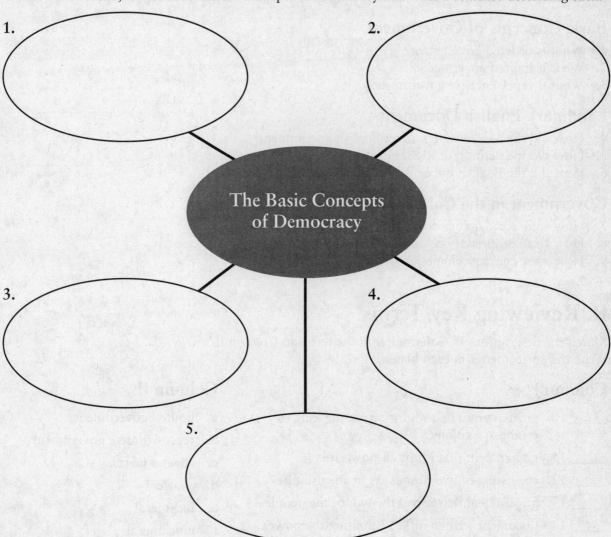

1.

2.

The Basic Concepts
of Democracy

3.

4.

5.

B. Reviewing Key Terms

Answer the following questions on a separate sheet of paper.

6. Explain the significance of the term *compromise* as it relates to problem-solving in a democratic society.

7. What are the four factors underlying the free enterprise system?

8. How does the law of supply and demand operate?

9. What is a mixed economy?

CHAPTER 2

Section 1: Guided Reading and Review
Our Political Beginnings

A. As You Read

As you read the section, answer the following questions on a separate sheet of paper.

Basic Concepts of Government

1. What is ordered government?
2. What is limited government?
3. What is representative government?

Landmark English Documents

4. How did the Magna Carta affect English government?
5. How did the Petition of Right affect English government?
6. How did the English Bill of Rights affect English government?

Government in the Colonies

7. How were royal colonies governed?
8. How were proprietary colonies governed?
9. How were charter colonies governed?

B. Reviewing Key Terms

Match the descriptions in Column I with the terms in Column II.
Write the correct letter in each blank.

Column I

_____ 10. written grant of authority from the king to establish a colony

_____ 11. government that is not all-powerful

_____ 12. consisting of two houses, as in a legislature

_____ 13. government that serves the will of the people

_____ 14. document written in 1215 limiting the power of the English monarchy

Column II

a. limited government

b. representative government

c. Magna Carta

d. charter

e. bicameral

f. unicameral

© Pearson Education, Inc.

Section 2: Guided Reading and Review
The Coming of Independence

CHAPTER 2

A. As You Read

The dates on the chart below indicate important developments and events related to American independence. As you read Section 2, fill in the chart by writing a brief description of the significance of each date listed.

Year/Date	Description of Event
1. 1643	
2. 1696	
3. 1754	
4. 1765	
5. 1770, March 5	
6. 1772	
7. 1773, December 16	
8. 1774, Spring	
9. 1774, September 5	
10. 1775, April 19	
11. 1775, May 10	
12. 1776, June 7	
13. 1776, July 2	
14. 1776, July 4	
15. 1781, March 1	

B. Reviewing Key Terms

Define the following key terms.

16. delegates_____

17. confederation _____

18. repeal _____

CHAPTER 2

Section 3: Guided Reading and Review
The Critical Period

A. As You Read

As you read Section 3, answer the questions below on a separate piece of paper or in the space provided.

The Articles of Confederation

1. Describe the structure of the government set up by the Articles of Confederation.

Fill in the chart below with the 10 powers granted to Congress under the Articles.

Congressional Powers Under the Articles of Confederation	
2._____	7._____
3._____	8._____
4._____	9._____
5._____	10. _____
6._____	11. _____

12. What obligations did States have to one another?

13. What obligations did States have to citizens?

14. What powers did Congress not have?

The Critical Period, the 1780s

15. What government action took place in response to Shays' Rebellion?

A Need for Stronger Government

16. What was the goal of the Constitutional Convention?

B. Reviewing Key Terms

Define the following key terms.

17. ratification _____

18. presiding officer _____

Section 4: Guided Reading and Review
Creating the Constitution

CHAPTER
2

A. As You Read

The chart below outlines the initial plans for a constitution and the "bundle of compromises" that resulted from the various plans. As you read Section 4, complete the chart by filling in the boxes provided.

Plan or Compromise	Provisions	Type of States That Benefited
Virginia Plan	1.	2.
New Jersey Plan	3.	4.
Connecticut Compromise	5.	6.
Three-Fifths Compromise	7.	8.
Commerce and Slave Trade Compromise	9.	10.

11. Name a group whose interests seem to have been ignored, or even harmed, by the compromises that created the Constitution. _____

B. Reviewing Key Terms

On a separate sheet of paper, use the key term below in a sentence that shows the meaning of the term.

12. Framers

Section 5: Guided Reading and Review
Ratifying the Constitution

A. As You Read

As you read the section, fill in the following outline by writing supporting details in the form of answers to questions 1–5.

The Fight for Ratification

1. What were the positions of each side toward ratification?

   a. Federalists: _____

   b. Anti-Federalists: _____

2. What were the five issues involved in the ratification debate?

   a. _____

   b. _____

   c. _____

   d. _____

   e. _____

3. On what two States did the success or failure of ratification depend?

   _____ and _____

Inaugurating the Government

4. Where was the first national capital located? _____

5. Who became the new nation's first President and Vice President?

   a. President: _____

   b. Vice President: _____

B. Reviewing Key Terms

Identify the following people as either a Federalist or an Anti-Federalist. On the spaces provided, write an A for Anti-Federalist or an F for Federalist.

6. James Madison _____

7. Patrick Henry _____

8. Alexander Hamilton _____

Section 1: Guided Reading and Review
The Six Basic Principles

CHAPTER 3

A. As You Read

As you read Section 1, fill in a description of each of the six basic principles of the Constitution, shown in the chart below.

Principle	Description
Popular Sovereignty	1.
Limited Government	2.
Separation of Powers	3.
Checks and Balances	4.
Judicial Review	5.
Federalism	6.

B. Reviewing Key Terms

Complete each sentence by writing the correct term in the blank provided.

7. The idea that government and its officers are always subject to— never above—the law is described as the _____.

8. The principle of _____ expresses the concept that government must be conducted according to constitutional principles.

9. Judicial review is the power to declare a government action that violates some provision of the Constitution to be _____.

10. The _____ is the brief introduction that begins the Constitution.

CHAPTER 3

Section 2: Guided Reading and Review
Formal Amendment

A. As You Read

As you read Section 2, answer the following questions.

Formal Amendment Process

1. What are the two steps involved in the first method of amending the Constitution?

    a. _____

    b. _____

2. What are the two steps involved in the second method of amending the Constitution?

    a. _____

    b. _____

3. What are the two steps involved in the third method of amending the Constitution?

    a. _____

    b. _____

4. What are the two steps involved in the fourth method of amending the Constitution?

    a. _____

    b. _____

The 27 Amendments

5. What is the Bill of Rights? _____

   _____

6. Which amendments were results of the Civil War? _____

   _____

B. Reviewing Key Terms

Use each key term below in a sentence that reflects the meaning of the term.

7. amendment _____

8. formal amendment _____

Section 3: Guided Reading and Review
Constitutional Change By Other Means

As You Read

As you read Section 3, complete the chart below by writing a brief definition of each method of informal constitutional change shown, and by giving an example of each.

Basic Legislation
1. Definition: _____
_____
2. Example: _____
_____

Executive Action
3. Definition: _____
_____
4. Example: _____
_____

Constitutional Change

Court Decisions
5. Definition: _____
_____
6. Example: _____
_____

Party Practices
9. Definition: _____
_____
10. Example: _____
_____

Custom
7. Definition: _____
_____
8. Example: _____
_____

B. Reviewing Key Terms

Define the following key terms.

11. treaty _____

12. executive agreement _____

13. senatorial courtesy _____

CHAPTER 4

Section 1: Guided Reading and Review
Federalism: The Division of Power

A. As You Read

As you read Section 1, write N in the first box provided if the power given belongs ONLY to the National Government, S if it belongs ONLY to the States, or B if it belongs to both. In the second box, write whether any power belonging to the National Government is an example of an expressed, implied, or inherent power.

Power	National (N), State (S), or Both(B)	Expressed, Implied, or Inherent
1. collect taxes		
2. build an interstate highway system		
3. regulate immigration		
4. license doctors		
5. make treaties		
6. maintain armed forces		
7. declare war		
8. deport alien		
9. prohibit racial discrimination in access to restaurants		
10. set up public school systems		
11. punish crimes		
12. coin money		
13. regulate the sale of liquor		
14. regulate interstate commerce		

B. Reviewing Key Terms

Complete each sentence by writing the correct term in the blank provided.

15. A system of government in which powers are divided between a central government and several regional governments is called _____.

16. The _____ powers are those set aside for the States.

17. The _____ between the National Government and the States was spelled out in the Bill of Rights.

NAME_____ CLASS _____ DATE _____

Section 2: Guided Reading and Review
The National Government and the 50 States

A. As You Read

As you read Section 2, answer the following questions on the lines provided.

The Nation's Obligations to the States

1. A republican form of government is _____.

2. Three obligations the Constitution places on the National Government for the benefit of the States are:
   a. _____
   b. _____
   c. _____

Admitting New States

3. A congressional act directing a territory that wants to become a State to frame a proposed State constitution is called _____.

4. A congressional law that agrees to grant statehood is _____
_____.

Cooperative Federalism

5. The general term for federal money or resources granted to States or local governments is
_____.

6. An example of a way that States aid the National Government is _____
_____.

B. Reviewing Key Terms

Match the descriptions in Column I with the terms in Column II.
Write the correct letter in each blank.

Column I

_____ 7. federal money granted to a State for a specific purpose

_____ 8. federal money given to States or other local governments with fewer-than-usual strings attached

_____ 9. federal aid program in place from 1972–1987 in which Congress gave a share of federal tax revenue to the States

_____ 10. federal money given to private agencies, States, or local governments that apply for it

Column II

a. revenue sharing

b. categorical grant

c. project grant

d. block grant

© Pearson Education, Inc.

Guided Reading and Review   **Chapter 4 29**

CHAPTER 4

Section 3: Guided Reading and Review
Interstate Relations

A. As You Read

The chart below will help you organize information on interstate relations. As you read Section 3, write the answer for each question in the spaces provided.

Interstate Relations
1. **Interstate Compacts** Why might States feel the need to form compacts with other States?   _____   _____
2. **Full Faith and Credit** What are three areas in which States give full faith and credit to citizens of other States? _____   _____
3. **Extradition** What is extradition? _____   _____   _____
4. **Privileges and Immunities** What is an example of a reasonable discrimination a State may exercise against a citizen of another State? _____   _____   _____

B. Reviewing Key Terms

Define the following terms in the space provided.

5. interstate compact _____

6. Full Faith and Credit Clause _____

7. Privileges and Immunities Clause _____

Section 1: Guided Reading and Review
Parties and What They Do

A. As You Read

As you read Section 1, write the correct answers in the blanks provided on the chart below.

Functions of Political Parties		
Function	**Description**	**Explanation**
1. _____	selecting candidates	The activity that sets political parties apart from other political groups
Informing and activating supporters	Inform people and activate their interests in public affairs.	Parties share this function with 2. _____ and 3. _____ groups.
Bonding agent	Tries to choose candidates who are 4. _____ and of good character.	After candidates are elected, the party prods them to do well or suffer in the next 5. _____
Governing	Helps 6. _____ and executive branches work together.	Most appointments to executive branch are made on basis of 7. _____, or allegiance to a political party.
8. _____	Party that is 9. _____ _____ criticizes the party that controls the government.	The loyal opposition urges votes to 10. _____ _____

B. Reviewing Key Terms

Complete each sentence by writing the correct term in the blank provided.

11. All _____ can be defined as groups of persons who join together because they want to gain control of the government through winning elections.

12. Allegiance to a political party is known as _____.

13. In the United States, the major _____ are the Democrats and the Republicans.

14. The party that controls the executive branch is known as the _____.

CHAPTER 5

Section 2: Guided Reading and Review
The Two-Party System

A. As You Read

As you read Section 2, fill in the blanks below explaining how each factor contributes to the stability of the two-party system in the United States.

1. Historical Basis: _____

_____

2. Tradition: _____

_____

3. Electoral System: _____

_____

4. Ideological Consensus: _____

_____

B. Reviewing Key Terms

Define the following terms.

5. minor party _____

6. two-party system _____

7. single-member district _____

8. plurality _____

9. pluralistic society _____

10. consensus _____

11. multiparty _____

12. one-party system _____

A. As You Read

On a separate sheet of paper, draw a chart like the one shown. Fill in the chart as you read Section 3.

	Period of Dominance (if any)	Supporters	Leaders
Federalists	1.	2.	3.
Jeffersonian Republicans	4.	5.	6.
Jacksonian Democrats	7.	8.	9.
Whigs	10.	11.	12.
Republicans	13.	14.	15.
Post-Civil War Democrats	16.	17.	18.
New Deal Democrats	19.	20.	21.

On a separate sheet of paper, describe the major issues for each of the following periods.

22. Era of the Democrats, 1800–1860
23. Era of the Republicans, 1860–1932
24. Return of the Democrats, 1932–1968

B. Reviewing Key Terms

On a separate sheet of paper define the following terms.

25. incumbent
26. faction
27. electorate
28. sectionalism

© Pearson Education, Inc.

CHAPTER 5

Section 4: Guided Reading and Review
The Minor Parties

A. As You Read

As you read Section 4, define and give examples of the four types of minor parties on the chart below.

	Definition	Examples
Ideological Parties	1.	2.
Single-Issue Parties	3.	4.
Economic Protest Parties	5.	6.
Splinter Parties	7.	8.

Answer the following questions on a separate sheet of paper.

9. What tends to happen to single-issue parties?

10. Which type of minor party has been most successful in winning votes?

11. Which type of minor party has been the longest lived?

12. What useful functions have minor parties performed in American history?

B. Reviewing Key Terms

Decide whether each of the following theoretical parties is an example of an ideological party, a single-issue party, an economic protest party, or a splinter party. Write the correct term in the blank provided.

_____ 13. The "Free Choice" party is formed by people intent on legalizing the use of marijuana for medical purposes.

_____ 14. A group of Democrats, dissatisfied with the party's moderate nominee, decides to form a new "People's Rights" party to back their more liberal leader, Henry J. Smith.

_____ 15. A group of angry Midwestern farmers and laborers forms the "Working People's" party, calling for higher tariffs, higher farm subsidies, and congressional term limitations.

_____ 16. The "Socialist Justice" party calls for a complete overhaul of the American political, economic, and legal systems.

_____ 17. The "Equity" party works for an end to affirmative action programs.

Section 5: Guided Reading and Review
Party Organization

A. As You Read

As you read Section 5, complete the chart below by supplying the missing information in the blanks provided.

National Party Machinery		
Mechanism	**Term or when it takes place**	**Role**
National Convention	1. _____	2. _____
National Committee	3. _____	4. _____
National Chairperson	5. _____	6. _____
Congressional Campaign	7. _____	8. _____

Complete each sentence by writing the correct term in the blank provided.

9. Two factors that contribute to the decentralization of parties are _____ and _____.

10. The party out of power operates at a disadvantage because it has no leader comparable to _____.

11. In recent years, there has been a sharp rise in the number of voters who identify themselves as _____.

B. Reviewing Key Terms

On a separate sheet of paper, define the following terms.

12. ward

13. precinct

14. split-ticket voting

CHAPTER 6

Section 1: Guided Reading and Review
The Right to Vote

A. As You Read

The chart below illustrates the expansion of suffrage. As you read Section 1, fill in the boxes provided by describing the portion of the American population that was qualified to vote at the time given.

1. _____
   the Constitution   1789

2. _____
   dropped religious & property qualifications   1850

3. _____
   15th Amendment   1870

4. _____
   19th Amendment   1920

5. _____
   Civil Rights Movement   1960s

6. _____
   26th Amendment   1971

Write the correct term in the blank provided.

During the last two hundred years, Americans have broadened the right (7.) _____ by eliminating barriers based on (8.) _____ belief, (9.) _____ ownership, (10.) _____ payment, race, and (11.) _____. At the same time, the (12.) _____ Government has assumed a greater role in deciding who can vote and how elections should be run.

B. Reviewing Key Terms

Match the descriptions in Column I with the terms in Column II. Write the correct letter in each blank. You may use two terms to answer one question.

Column I

_____ 13. the right to vote

_____ 14. the potential voting population

Column II

a. electorate

b. franchise

c. suffrage

© Pearson Education, Inc.

Section 2: Guided Reading and Review
Voter Qualifications

A. As You Read

As you read Section 2, answer the following questions in the space provided.

1. According to the Constitution, can aliens vote? _____

2. Do any State governments today allow aliens to vote? _____

3. What are the two reasons that States adopted residency requirements?

   a. _____

   b. _____

4. What is the longest period of residence that any State today requires before permitting new residents to vote? _____

5. What is the oldest minimum age a State can set for voters? _____

6. What kinds of information are voters usually asked to give when they register to vote? ____
   _____

7. a. Why do some people argue that voter registration ought to be abolished? _____

   b. Why do others believe registration is important? _____
   _____

8. What were the three provisions of the Motor Voter Law? _____
   _____

9. Why were literacy tests abolished? _____
   _____

10. In what region of the country was the poll tax once used? Why was it abolished? _____
    _____
    _____

11. What groups of persons are widely barred from voting? _____
    _____

B. Reviewing Key Terms

Complete each sentence by writing the correct term in the blank provided.

12. _____ is the ability to read or write.

13. A _____ was a sum of money that had to be paid by the voter at the time he or she cast a ballot.

14. _____ is a procedure for voter identification.

15. Election officials are regularly supposed to _____ their _____ of the names of those who no longer meet voting requirements.

16. Most States prohibit _____, people who live there for a short time, from being considered legal residents.

CHAPTER 6

Section 3: Guided Reading and Review
Suffrage and Civil Rights

A. As You Read

As you read Section 3, complete the paragraphs below by writing the correct answers in the blanks provided.

THE 15TH AMENDMENT was ratified in (1.) _____. It states that no citizen can be denied suffrage on the basis of (2.) _____, color, or previous condition of (3.) _____. Although this amendment was intended to enfranchise (4.) _____ men, in fact it was not enforced for almost 100 years.

THE CIVIL RIGHTS ACT OF 1957 set up the (5.) _____ and gave the attorney general the right to seek federal (6.) _____ to prevent actions that interfered with the voting rights of qualified citizens.

THE CIVIL RIGHTS ACT OF 1960 provided for the appointment of federal (7.) _____ _____. Their duty was to make sure that qualified citizens were allowed to (8.) _____ and (9.) _____ in federal elections.

THE CIVIL RIGHTS ACT OF 1964 forbade discriminatory (10.) _____ requirements. It relied heavily on the use of the (11.) _____ system to overcome racial discrimination. Its shortcomings became clear when Martin Luther (12.) _____ organized a voter registration drive in the city of (13.) _____. Efforts to register African-American voters were met with violent opposition.

THE VOTING RIGHTS ACT OF 1965 attacked the use of the (14.) _____ tax and (15.) _____ tests. It authorized the appointment of (16.) _____ in any State or county in which less than (17.) _____ of the electorate had been registered or (18.) _____ in the 1964 elections. In 1975 the law was extended to cover States and counties in which more than (19.) _____ percent of the adult population belongs to the following groups: (20.) _____ _____

B. Reviewing Key Terms

Write the correct definition for each of the following terms on a separate sheet of paper and tell why they were important.

21. gerrymandering
22. injunction
23. preclearance

Section 4: Guided Reading and Review
Voter Behavior

CHAPTER
6

A. As You Read

As you read the section, fill in the answers to the questions below.

1. What type of election years have the highest voter turnout? _____

2. What is "ballot fatigue"? _____

3. What is the largest group of "cannot-voters"? _____

4. Why do some nonvoters deliberately choose to not vote? _____
_____

5. What is "time-zone fallout"? _____

6. What is the chief reason that most nonvoters do not vote? _____
_____

7. How do each of these factors affect the likelihood of whether people do or do not vote?

   a. level of income: _____

   b. occupation: _____

   c. education: _____

   d. age: _____

   e. gender: _____

   f. party identification: _____

Fill in the characteristics in the chart below to compare some factors that influence whether people are more likely to vote Democrat or Republican.

	Democrat	Republican
Income/Occupation	8.	9.
Education	10.	11.
Gender/Age	12.	13.
Religion	14.	15.
Ethnicity	16.	17.
Geography	18.	19.

B. Reviewing Key Terms

On a separate sheet of paper, define the following terms.

20. off-year election

21. political efficacy

22. political socialization

23. gender gap

24. party identification

25. straight-ticket voting

26. split-ticket voting

27. independents

CHAPTER 7

Section 1: Guided Reading and Review
The Nominating Process

A. As You Read

Complete the chart below as you read Section 1. For each nominating method, write when it came into use and the procedure for nominating candidates.

Nominating Method	How it Works
Self-Announcement	1.
Caucus	2.
Convention	3.
Direct Primary	4.
Closed Primary	5.
Open Primary	6.
Petition	7.

Answer the following questions on a separate sheet of paper.

8. Why is the nominating process particularly important in a two-party system?

9. What are some popular criticisms of the primary process?

B. Reviewing Key Terms

Read the statements below. If a statement is true, write T in the blank provided. If it is false, write F. Then rewrite the statement on a separate sheet of paper to make it true.

_____ 10. Nomination means the naming of candidates who will seek office.

_____ 11. During the early national period, major-party presidential candidates were nominated by State legislatures.

_____ 12. In a blanket primary, voters can nominate a Democratic and a Republican candidate for each office.

_____ 13. In States that require nominees to win a plurality of the popular vote, runoff primaries are sometimes needed.

_____ 14. In a nonpartisan election, candidates are not identified by party.

Section 2: Guided Reading and Review
Elections

A. As You Read

1. Write a brief paragraph summarizing the information given under the heading "The Administration of Elections."

Complete the chart below as you read Section 2. For each method of voting given, write its major features and any advantages or disadvantages of the methods.

Method of Voting	Features	Advantages/Disadvantages
Voice Voting	2.	3.
Early Paper Ballots	4.	5.
Australian Ballot	6.	7.
Office–Group Ballot	8.	9.
Party–Column Ballot	10.	11.
Vote by Mail	12.	13.
Online Voting	14.	15.

B. Reviewing Key Terms

On a separate sheet of paper, define the following terms.

16. absentee voting

17. coattail effect

18. precinct

19. polling place

20. ballot

Section 3: Guided Reading and Review
Money and Elections

A. As You Read

Fill in the spaces below to organize information about money and the election process. Under each main idea, write three supporting details from Section 3.

Main Idea A: Candidates spend a great deal of money on political campaigns.

1. _____

2. _____

3. _____

Main Idea B: Private donors come in many different shapes and sizes.

4. _____

5. _____

6. _____

7. _____

8. _____

Main Idea C: Laws that the Federal Election Commission (FEC) enforces cover four areas.

9. _____

10. _____

11. _____

12. _____

Main Idea D: There are three major loopholes in campaign finance laws.

13. _____

14. _____

15. _____

B. Reviewing Key Terms

On a separate sheet of paper, define the following terms.

16. political action committee

17. subsidy

18. soft money

19. hard money

Section 1: Guided Reading and Review
The Formation of Public Opinion

CHAPTER
8

A. As You Read

Complete the chart below as you read Section 1. For each source of information given, write the type of information that is communicated.

Factors that Shape Public Opinion	
Sources	Types of Information Communicated
The Family	1.
The Schools	2.
The Mass Media	3.
Peer Groups	4.
Opinion Leaders	5.
Historic Events	6.

Write the answers to questions 7 and 8 on a separate sheet of paper.

7. What does it mean to say that "many publics exists exist in the United States?"

8. Why are family and school particularly important in shaping people's political views?

B. Reviewing Key Terms

On a separate sheet of paper, define the following terms.

9. public affairs

10. public opinion

11. mass media

12. peer group

13. opinion leader

CHAPTER 8

Section 2: Guided Reading and Review
Measuring Public Opinion

A. As You Read

Complete the chart below as you read Section 2. Describe how each measure gauges public opinion and how accurate a measure it is.

Measure	How and How Well?
Elections	1.
Interest Groups	2.
Media	3.
Personal Contracts	4.
Polls	5.

List the five steps of the polling process. Give a brief description of each.

6. Step 1 _____
_____

7. Step 2 _____
_____

8. Step 3 _____
_____

9. Step 4 _____
_____

10. Step 5 _____
_____

B. Reviewing Key Terms

On a separate sheet of paper, use each term below in a sentence that shows the meaning of the term.

11. mandate

12. interest group

13. public opinion poll

14. straw vote

15. sample

16. random sample

17. quota sample

© Pearson Education, Inc.

NAME _____ CLASS _____ DATE _____

A. As You Read

Complete the chart below as you read Section 3. List the media in order of their degree of influence on public opinion and give examples of each.

Medium	Examples
1.	
2.	
3.	
4.	

Write the answers to questions 5–7 on the blanks provided.

5. How do the mass media help to shape the public agenda? _____
_____

6. How has television influenced each of the following?

   a. the power of political parties _____
_____

   b. political campaigns _____
_____

7. What factors limit the influence of the mass media? _____
_____

B. Reviewing Key Terms

On a separate sheet of paper, define the following terms.

  8. medium _____

  9. public agenda _____

10. sound bite _____

© Pearson Education, Inc.

CHAPTER 9

Section 1: Guided Reading and Review
The Nature of Interest Groups

A. As You Read

Use the information in Section 1 to fill in the following supporting facts under each main idea.

Main Idea A: Interest groups differ from political parties in several ways.

1. _____

2. _____

3. _____

Main Idea B: Interest groups have historically been regarded with suspicion.

4. James Madison warned against _____.

5. Madison hoped to moderate the power of interest groups through _____

_____.

Main Idea C: Interest groups fulfill many functions in American society.

6. _____

7. _____

8. _____

9. _____

10. _____

11. _____

Main Idea D: Interest groups also pose a number of problems for the United States.

12. _____

13. _____

14. _____

15. _____

B. Reviewing Key Terms

Define the terms listed below in the spaces provided.

16. interest group _____

17. public policy _____

18. public affairs _____

Section 2: Guided Reading and Review
Types of Interest Groups

CHAPTER 9

A. As You Read

1. On a separate sheet of paper, write four sentences summarizing the information given about interest groups under the heading "An American Tradition."

As you read Section 2, complete the chart below by filling in the type of interest group or examples of the type of interest group.

Type of Interest Group	Examples
Business Groups	2. _____
Labor Groups	3. _____
4. _____	National Grange, American Farm Bureau, National Farmers Union
Professional Groups	5. _____
6. _____	ACLU, Sierra Club, National Women's Political Caucus
7. _____	American Legion, Older Americans, Inc., NAACP
8. _____	National Council of Churches, American Jewish Congress, National Catholic Welfare Council
Public- Interest Groups	9. _____

B. Reviewing Key Terms

Match the groups in Column I with the interest group type in Column II.

Column I

_____ 10. a group that pushes for public policies that benefit most or all people in the country, regardless of whether they belong to or support the group

_____ 11. an interest group for a segment of the business community

_____ 12. an organization of workers who work in the same type of job or who work in the same industry

Column II

a. trade association

b. labor union

c. public-interest group

© Pearson Education, Inc.

CHAPTER 9

Section 3: Guided Reading and Review
Interest Groups at Work

A. As You Read

As you read Section 3, write three supporting details for each of the main ideas given.

Main Idea A: Interest groups try to influence public opinion.

1. _____
   _____

2. _____
   _____

3. _____
   _____

Main Idea B: Interest groups help and make use of political parties.

4. _____
   _____

5. _____
   _____

6. _____
   _____

Main Idea C: Lobbying involves many functions.

7. _____
   _____

8. _____
   _____

9. _____
   _____

B. Reviewing Key Terms

On a separate sheet of paper, define each key term below and use it in a sentence.

10. propaganda

11. single-interest group

12. lobbying

13. grass roots

© Pearson Education, Inc.

Section 1: Guided Reading and Review
The National Legislature

A. As You Read

The main points of Section 1 are supplied for you below in the form of questions. As you read the section, fill in the answers to the questions.

Two Houses of Congress

1. What is the historical reason for Americans choosing a bicameral system? _____

    _____

2. What is a practical reason for Americans choosing a bicameral system? _____

    _____

3. What is a theoretical reason for Americans choosing a bicameral system? _____

    _____

Terms and Sessions

4. What is a term of Congress? _____

    _____

5. What is a session of Congress? _____

    _____

6. How many sessions are there in a term of Congress? _____

B. Reviewing Key Terms

Define the following terms.

7. adjourn _____

8. special session _____

CHAPTER 10

Section 2: Guided Reading and Review
The House of Representatives

A. As You Read

Using information from this section, complete the chart below, which shows data related to the House of Representatives.

Characteristics of House	Description
1. Size	
2. Terms	
3. Date of election	

Characteristics of Its Members	Qualifications
4. Age	
5. Length of citizenship	
6. Residence	

B. Reviewing Key Terms

Define the following terms

7. gerrymandering _____

_____

8. reapportionment _____

9. off-year election _____

_____

Section 3: Guided Reading and Review
The Senate

CHAPTER
10

A. As You Read

Using information from this section, compare data about the Senate with data about the House by filling in the blanks in the chart below.

The Congress

Characteristic	House	Senate
Size	435	1. _____
Term Length	2 years	2. _____
Date of Elections	Tuesday following first Monday in November of each even-numbered year	3. _____ _____
Qualifications		
Age	At least 25 years	4. _____
Length of Citizenship	At least 7 years	5. _____
Residence	Inhabitant of the State	6. _____
How Chosen		
Originally	By voters in district	7. _____
Today	By voters in district	8. _____

B. Reviewing Key Terms

Complete each sentence by writing the correct term in the blank provided.

9. The Senate is a _____, that is, all of its seats are never up for election at the same time.

10. _____ are the people and interests the senators represent.

CHAPTER
10

Section 4: Guided Reading and Review
The Members of Congress

A. As You Read

As you read Section 4, answer the questions below on the roles played by members of Congress and the compensation and privileges of the job.

Roles Played by a Member of Congress

1. **Legislator:** What does a legislator do? _____

2. **Committee member:** What do members do as part of a congressional committee? _____

_____

3. **Trustee:** How does a member of Congress act as a trustee? _____

_____

4. **Delegate:** How does a member of Congress act as a delegate? _____

_____

5. **Partisan:** How does a member of Congress act as a partisan? _____

_____

6. **Politico:** How does a member of Congress act as a politico? _____

_____

Compensation and Privileges

7. **Salary:** What is the current salary of a member of Congress? _____

8. **Nonsalary compensation:** What are some fringe benefits for members of Congress? _____

_____

9. **Privileges:** To what does the phrase "cloak of legislative immunity" refer? _____

_____

B. Reviewing Key Terms

Define the following terms.

10. constituency _____

11. oversight function _____

© Pearson Education, Inc.

Section 1: Guided Reading and Review
The Scope of Congressional Powers

A. As You Read

Compare the concepts of strict and liberal constructionism by completing the chart below.

Construction of the Constitution		
	Strict	**Liberal**
Definition	1. _____	2. _____
Major proponent	3. _____	4. _____
Attitude toward implied powers	5. _____	6. _____
Attitude toward national power	7. _____	8. _____
Attitude toward State power	9. _____	10. _____

B. Reviewing Key Terms

Complete each sentence by writing the correct term in the blank provided.

11. The Constitution gives powers to the Congress in three ways:

   a. through the _____, or clearly stated, powers,

   b. through the _____, powers (powers deducted from the clearly stated powers),

   c. through the _____ powers, those possessed by all sovereign states.

CHAPTER 11

Section 2: Guided Reading and Review
The Expressed Powers of Money and Commerce

A. As You Read

Complete the chart below showing the major powers granted to Congress by the Constitution in the areas of money and commerce.

Congress's Constitutional Powers of Money and Commerce	
Power	**Allows Congress to...**
Taxation	1. _____ _____
Borrowing	2. _____ _____
Commerce	3. _____ _____
Currency	4. _____ _____
Bankruptcy	5. _____ _____

B. Reviewing Key Terms

Define the following terms.

6. tax _____

_____

7. indirect tax _____

_____

8. deficit financing _____

_____

9. public debt _____

_____

10. legal tender _____

_____

11. bankruptcy _____

_____

Section 3: Guided Reading and Review
Other Expressed Powers

CHAPTER 11

A. As You Read

Fill in the supporting points in the outline below in the form of answers to the questions.

Foreign Relations Powers

1. Which parts of the National Government share the power in the field of foreign affairs? _____
_____

2. Which part is primarily responsible for conducting foreign relations? _____

3. What is the role of the States in foreign affairs and why? _____
_____

War Powers

4. Who has the power to declare war? _____

5. What did the War Powers Resolution of 1973 state? _____
_____

Other Expressed Powers

6. What power gives Congress the right to make laws regulating mailing? _____
_____

7. What is the role of the National Institute of Standards and Technology in fulfilling an expressed
power? _____
_____

Judicial Powers

8. The Constitution specifically mentions the following four kinds of federal crimes:
   a. _____
   b. _____
   c. _____
   d. _____

9. Which part of the National Government has the expressed power of creating and providing for
the organization of federal courts?_____

B. Reviewing Key Terms

Complete each sentence by writing the correct term in the blank provided.

10. _____ is the process of making non-citizens into citizens.

11. A _____ protects the right of an author over original writings.

12. A _____ protects an inventor's rights to inventions.

13. _____ is the right of a government to take private property for public use.

Section 4: Guided Reading and Review
The Implied Powers

A. As You Read

Complete the following time line by inserting the correct events described in Section 4 in the spaces indicated. Then answer the questions that follow.

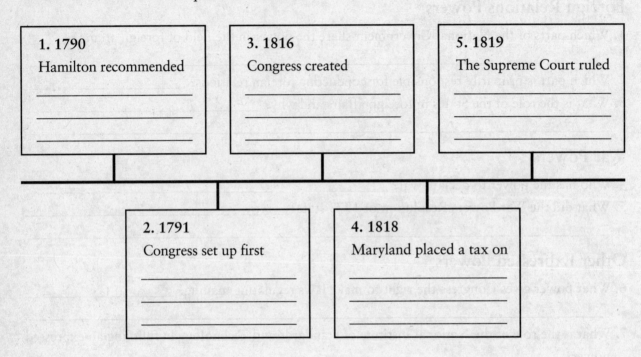

1. 1790
Hamilton recommended
_____
_____
_____

3. 1816
Congress created
_____
_____
_____

5. 1819
The Supreme Court ruled
_____
_____
_____

2. 1791
Congress set up first
_____
_____
_____

4. 1818
Maryland placed a tax on
_____
_____
_____

B. Reviewing Key Terms

6. Explain why the Necessary and Proper Clause has often been called the Elastic Clause.

_____
_____
_____
_____
_____

7. Why does Congress have the power to appropriate funds for various purposes? _____

_____
_____
_____
_____

Section 5: Guided Reading and Review
The Nonlegislative Powers

A. As You Read

On a separate sheet of paper, answer the following questions as you read Section 5.

Constitutional Amendments

1. What are two ways Congress may propose an amendment to the Constitution?
2. What are some current issues that many Americans have thought worthy of constitutional amendment?

Electoral Duties

3. What electoral duty does the House have?
4. What electoral duty does the Senate have?

Impeachment

5. What role does the House have in the impeachment process?
6. What role does the Senate have in the impeachment process?

Executive Powers

7. What are the two executive powers possessed by the Senate?
8. What is "senatorial courtesy"?

Investigatory Powers

9. What is the usual forum for congressional investigations?
10. What are some reasons for congressional investigations?

B. Reviewing Key Terms

Complete the sentence by writing the correct term in the blank provided.

11. It is the Senate, not the House, which has sole power to _____ President, Vice President, and all civil officers of the United States.

12. Congress may _____ someone by issuing a formal condemnation of the individual's actions.

CHAPTER 12

Section 1: Guided Reading and Review
Congress Organizes

A. As You Read

Complete the graphic organizer below showing the organization of the House of Representatives and the Senate. Fill in the presiding officers that are missing from the organizer and code each box, using the key provided, to indicate whether each officer is a party officer, an official presiding officer, or both.

House
Presiding Officer and Party Leader
1. _____

Party Officers	
2. _____	3. _____
4. _____	5. _____

Senate
Presiding Officers

6. _____	7. _____

Party Officers	
8. _____	9. _____
10. _____	11. _____

B. Reviewing Key Terms

Answer the following questions on a separate piece of paper.

12. What are the functions of the Speaker of the House?

13. What are the functions of the president of the Senate?

14. What are the functions of the floor leaders and their whips in both houses?

© Pearson Education, Inc.

Section 2: Guided Reading and Review
Committees in Congress

A. As You Read

Complete the graphic organizer below by answering the questions about congressional committees.

Standing Committees

1. What is a standing committee? _____

_____

2. What are the committees' functions? _____

_____

3. Give 3 examples of such committees.

_____

_____

_____

Select Committees

4. What is a select committee?_____

_____

5. What does a select committee do? _____

_____

6. Give 2 examples of a select committee from 1987._____

_____

_____

Types of Congressional Committees

Joint Committees

7. What is a joint committee? _____

_____

8. What does a joint committee do? _____

_____

9. Give 3 examples of a joint committee.

_____

_____

_____

Conference Committees

10. What is a conference committee? _____

_____

_____

11. What does a conference committee do?

_____

_____

_____

B. Reviewing Key Terms

Answer the question below on a separate sheet of paper.

12. How does the House Rules Committee act as a "traffic cop" in the lower house?

CHAPTER 12

Section 3: Guided Reading and Review
How a Bill Becomes a Law: The House

A. As You Read

Fill in the information below by writing the answers in the blanks provided.

1. Most bills are introduced in Congress by _____

_____

2. A bill is _____

3. A resolution deals with _____

4. A joint resolution is like a bill because _____

_____

5. A concurrent resolution deals with _____

_____

6. At a first reading of a bill, the clerk _____

_____

7. Five courses of action a committee may take on a bill are:_____

_____

_____

_____

_____

8. Four types of votes in the House are: _____

_____

_____

_____

9. After a bill has been passed and signed by the Speaker, _____

_____

_____

B. Reviewing Key Terms

Define the following terms.

10. rider _____

11. quorum _____

12. concurrent resolution_____

13. discharge petition _____

14. Committee of the Whole _____

_____

© Pearson Education, Inc.

Section 4: Guided Reading and Review
The Bill in the Senate

CHAPTER **12**

A. As You Read

Fill in the blanks on the flowchart below that outlines the movements of a bill through the Senate.

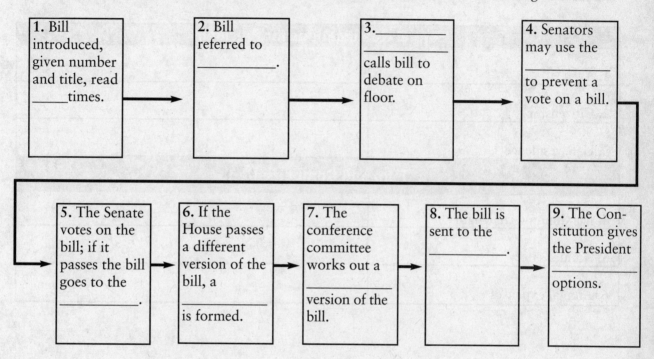

1. Bill introduced, given number and title, read _____ times.

2. Bill referred to _____.

3. _____ _____ calls bill to debate on floor.

4. Senators may use the _____ to prevent a vote on a bill.

5. The Senate votes on the bill; if it passes the bill goes to the _____.

6. If the House passes a different version of the bill, a _____ is formed.

7. The conference committee works out a _____ version of the bill.

8. The bill is sent to the _____.

9. The Constitution gives the President _____ options.

B. Reviewing Key Terms

Complete each sentence by writing the correct term in the blank provided.

10. The Senate is reluctant to use _____ to limit debate.

11. In practice, just the threat of a _____, an attempt to "talk a bill to death," can result in the Senate's failure to consider certain bills.

12. By not acting on a bill sent by Congress within 10 days of adjourning, the President performs a _____ .

13. The President may _____ a bill sent to him by Congress by refusing to sign it.

CHAPTER 13

Section 1: Guided Reading and Review
The President's Job Description

A. As You Read

As you read Section 1, fill in a brief description for each of the roles of the President given below.

Formal Qualifications for President	
1. Age	
2. Citizenship	
3. U. S. residence	
Term and Compensation	
4. Maximum term length	
5. Annual salary	
6. Annual expenses	

B. Reviewing Key Terms

Match the descriptions in Column 1 with the terms in Column II. Write the correct letter in each blank.

Column I

_____ 7. chief of state

_____ 8. chief executive

_____ 9. chief administrator

_____ 10. chief diplomat

_____ 11. commander in chief

_____ 12. chief legislator

_____ 13. chief of party

_____ 14. chief citizen

Column II

a. proposes laws to Congress

b. ceremonial head of government

c. represents the American people

d. heads the federal bureaucracy

e. determines foreign policy

f. leads his or her political party

g. commands the armed forces

h. sees that the nation's laws are carried out

Section 2: Guided Reading and Review

Presidential Succession and the Vice Presidency

A. As You Read

As you read Section 2, use the chart below to write the correct order of succession to the presidency.

The Order of Succession to the Presidency

1. _____

2. _____

3. _____

4. _____

5. _____

Answer the following questions in the blanks provided.

6. How does the Constitution provide for situations in which the President is disabled? _____
_____

7. What duties are given to the Vice President by the Constitution? _____
_____

8. How are Vice Presidents usually selected? _____
_____

9. How can a vacancy in the vice presidency be filled? _____
_____

B. Reviewing Key Terms

Write the definition of each term in the blank provided.

10. presidential succession _____
_____
_____

11. balance the ticket _____
_____
_____

CHAPTER 13

Section 3: Guided Reading and Review
Presidential Selection: The Framers' Plan

A. As You Read

As you read Section 3, answer the following questions on the lines provided.

1. What were three methods of presidential election discussed by the Framers? _____

   _____

   _____

2. How did the Framers arrange for the electors to choose the President and Vice President?

   _____

3. Why did the Framers choose this method of electing the President? What kind of person did

   they envision as an elector? _____

4. How did the rise of political parties affect the electoral college? _____

   _____

5. How did the election of 1800 lead to passage of the 12th Amendment? _____

   _____

B. Reviewing Key Terms

Use each key term below in a sentence that shows the meaning of the term.

6. presidential electors _____

   _____

7. electoral college _____

   _____

Section 4: Guided Reading and Review
Presidential Nominations

A. As You Read

Complete the outline below by filling in the blanks to complete the sentences.

The Role of Conventions

1. From 1800 to 1824, presidential candidates were chosen by _____
   _____.

2. In 1832, that system was replaced by the _____.

3. Today, the Democratic and Republican parties allot each State a number of party delegates based on the State's electoral vote and _____

4. The procedure for selecting delegates in a primary is governed by State laws and/or _____
   _____.

Presidential Primaries

5. A State's presidential primary may either be a process to _____ or to indicate _____.

6. Winner-take-all primaries have nearly disappeared in favor of _____.

7. The few States that do not hold primaries choose delegates in _____ and
   _____.

The National Convention

8. The _____ is the statement of a party's basic principles.

9. The _____ is the speech that is usually given on the first day of a convention.

Who Is Nominated?

10. An _____ President who wants to run again is usually nominated.

11. The greatest number of people who have been nominated for President have previously served as _____.

B. Reviewing Key Terms

Define the following terms.

12. presidential primary _____
    _____
    _____

13. proportional representation _____
    _____
    _____

CHAPTER 13

Section 5: Guided Reading and Review
The Election

A. As You Read

Using information from Section 5, complete the chart below, which shows different plans for electing the President.

Actual or Proposed System	How it Works	Flaws
Electoral College	1.	2.
District Plan	3.	4.
Proportional Plan	5.	6.
Direct Popular Election	7.	8.
National Bonus Plan	9.	10.

11. In which three elections of the past has the winner of the popular vote failed to win the electoral vote for the presidency? _____ _____ _____

B. Reviewing Key Terms

Define the following key term.

12. electorate _____

_____

Section 1: Guided Reading and Review
The Growth of Presidential Power

CHAPTER
14

A. As You Read

As you read Section 1, complete the sentences below.

Article II

1. Article II is known as the _____ because it establishes the presidency.

2. Article II establishes the following presidential powers:

   a. _____

   b. _____

   c. _____

   d. _____

   e. _____

   f. _____

3. Beginning at the Philadelphia Convention in 1787, there has been a struggle between those who want a _____ and those who want a _____.

Why Presidential Power Has Grown

4. Throughout American history, those who want a _____ have usually prevailed.

5. One reason for the growth of presidential power has been the nation's increasingly complex _____.

6. The frequent need for _____ has also strengthened presidential power.

7. Even _____ has strengthened the presidency by passing laws that added to the activities of the executive branch.

The Presidential View

8. Some strong, effective Presidents have stated the _____ theory, which takes a broad view of their powers.

9. Critics of strong presidential power compare the President to an emperor, calling a strong presidency a(n) _____.

B. Reviewing Key Terms

Define the following key term on the lines provided.

10. mass media _____

_____

_____

CHAPTER 14 — Section 2: Guided Reading and Review
The President's Executive Powers

A. As You Read

As you read Section 2, use the chart below to indicate whether the power is implied or expressed and to describe each executive power shown.

The Executive Powers of the President		
Function	**Implied or Expressed?**	**Gives the President Power to...**
Executing the Law	1.	2.
The Ordinance Power	3.	4.
The Appointment Power	5.	6.
The Removal Power	7.	8.

B. Reviewing Key Terms

Use each key term below in a sentence that shows the meaning of the term.

9. oath of office _____

_____

10. executive order _____

_____

Section 3: Guided Reading and Review
Diplomatic and Military Powers

A. As You Read

As you read Section 3, complete the outline by filling in the blanks.

The Power to Make Treaties

1. A treaty is a formal agreement between _____.

2. After the President negotiates a treaty, the _____ must approve it by a
   _____ vote.

3. Presidents Tyler and McKinley encouraged Congress to pass a _____ to
   annex territory after the approval of a treaty had been defeated in the Senate.

Executive Agreements

4. An executive agreement is _____.

5. One difference between an executive agreement and a treaty is that an executive agreement
   does not require _____.

The Power of Recognition

6. By exercising the power of recognition, the President acknowledges the
   _____ of another country and its government.

7. Prompt recognition of a country or its government may _____ its existence.

8. Displeasure with another country's conduct may be shown by the President's asking for
   _____.

9. The most serious diplomatic rebuke one nation may give another is the _____
   _____.

Commander in Chief

10. The President's powers as commander in chief are almost _____.

11. Presidents have used the armed forces in combat abroad without _____.

12. A President's power as commander in chief is greatest during _____.

13. Congress passed the War Powers Resolution in 1973 to limit the President's war-making
    powers in response to _____.

14. The constitutionality of the War Powers Resolution remains _____.

B. Reviewing Key Terms

Define the following term.

15. *persona non grata* _____

CHAPTER 14

Section 4: Guided Reading and Review
Legislative and Judicial Powers

A. As You Read

As you read Section 4, complete the outline on legislative powers by writing the correct words or phrases in the blanks.

1. Using his message power, the President regularly sends these three major messages to Congress:

   a. _____

   b. _____

   c. _____

2. The President's four options in dealing with a measure passed by Congress are:

   a. _____

   b. _____

   c. _____

   d. _____

3. Throughout history Presidents have requested the veto power to include the

   _____ that would allow them to cancel specific dollar amounts in spending.

4. Article II, Section 3 allows the President to call Congress into _____.

5. No President has yet used the power to _____ Congress.

B. Reviewing Key Terms

Match the descriptions in Column I with the terms in Column II. Write the correct letter in each blank.

Column I

_____ 6. a general pardon offered to a group of lawbreakers

_____ 7. mercy or leniency given in cases involving federal offenses

_____ 8. a postponement of the execution of a sentence imposed by a court

_____ 9. a reduction in the severity of a sentence or fine imposed by a court

_____ 10. legal forgiveness of a crime

Column II

a. commutation

b. clemency

c. amnesty

d. reprieve

e. pardon

© Pearson Education, Inc.

Section 1: Guided Reading and Review
The Federal Bureaucracy

A. As You Read

Fill in the outline below by answering the questions in the spaces provided.

What Is a Bureaucracy?

1. Name the three main characteristics of a bureaucracy and explain why each is important.

   a. _____

   b. _____

   c. _____

Major Elements of the Federal Bureaucracy

2. How does the Constitution make reference to a federal bureaucracy? _____

   _____

3. Which two departments does the Constitution anticipate?

   a. _____   b. _____

The Name Game

Define the following titles of executive branch units and give one example of each unit. You may use section content and the chart on Student Edition page 417.

4. department _____

   _____

5. agency _____

   _____

6. administration _____

7. commission _____

8. corporation/authority _____

   _____

Staff and Line Agencies

Define the following terms and give an example of each.

9. staff agency _____

10. line agency _____

B. Reviewing Key Terms

On a separate sheet of paper, use each key term in a sentence that shows the meaning of the term.

11. bureaucrat   12. administration

CHAPTER 15

Section 2: Guided Reading and Review
The Executive Office of the President

A. As You Read

As you read Section 2, use the chart below to organize information about the Executive Office of the President (EOP). Describe the major function of each agency in the Executive Office shown in boxes 1–11.

Executive Office Agencies	Function
1. White House Executive Office	
2. National Security Council	
3. Office of Management and Budget	
4. Office of National Drug Control Policy	
5. Council of Economic Advisers	
6. Office of Policy Development	
7. Council of Environmental Equality	
8. Office of the Vice President	
9. Office of the U.S. Trade Representatives	
10. Office of Science and Technology	
11. Office of Administration	

B. Reviewing Key Terms

Define each of the following terms in the space provided.

12. federal budget _____

13. fiscal year _____

14. domestic affairs _____

Section 3: Guided Reading and Review
The Executive Departments

A. As You Read

As you read Section 3, fill in the answers to the questions below.

1. What is another name for the executive departments? _____

2. What is the title for the heads of most executive departments? _____

3. What is the title for the head of the Department of Justice? _____

4. What are the two main duties of the heads of the executive departments? _____
   _____
   _____

5. How many executive departments are there today? _____

6. About what percentage of employees of executive departments are career people, not political appointees? _____

7. About what percentage of employees of executive departments do not work in Washington, D.C.? _____

8. What is the role of the Cabinet? _____
   _____

9. What is the process for appointing the heads of executive departments? _____
   _____

10. What is the basis for the existence of the Cabinet? _____

11. When was the first woman appointed to the Cabinet? _____

12. What President appointed the greatest number of women and minority members to the Cabinet? _____

B. Reviewing Key Terms

Define the following term in the space provided.

13. executive department _____
    _____
    _____

CHAPTER 15

Section 4: Guided Reading and Review
Independent Agencies

A. As You Read

As you read Section 4, fill in the chart below describing the functions of the three types of independent agencies, and giving at least two examples of each type of agency.

Independent Agencies		
Type of Agency	**Functions**	**Examples**
Independent Executive Agencies	1.	2.
Independent Regulatory Commissions	3.	4.
Government Corporations	5.	6.

B. Reviewing Key Terms

Complete each sentence by writing the correct term or phrase in the blank provided.

7. The term independent agencies means that the agencies are not part of _____
_____ .

8. Independent regulatory commissions are _____ bodies, which means they have the power to make rules and regulations.

9. They also have quasi-judicial powers, which they exercise by _____
_____ .

© Pearson Education, Inc.

Section 5: Guided Reading and Review **CHAPTER 15**
The Civil Service

A. As You Read

As you read Section 5, answer the questions below about changes in the manner of choosing federal employees.

1. How did the first Presidents choose federal officials? _____
_____

2. How did Jackson choose federal officials? _____
_____

3. What government action began civil service reform and how did it work? _____
_____

4. What two agencies run and oversee the civil service system today? Describe the functions of
each. _____
_____
_____
_____

5. How has the Federal Employees Political Activities Act of 1993 relaxed restrictions placed by
the Hatch Act of 1939? _____
_____
_____
_____

B. Reviewing Key Terms

Use each key term below in a sentence that shows the meaning of the term.

6. spoils system _____
_____

7. patronage _____

8. register_____
_____

9. bipartisan _____
_____

10. civil service _____
_____

CHAPTER 16

Section 1: Guided Reading and Review
Taxes

A. As You Read

Write the answers to the questions below in the blanks provided.

The Power to Tax

1. What are the expressed constitutional limitations to the power to tax?
   a. _____
   b. _____
   c. _____
   d. _____

2. What is the implied limitation on the power to tax State and local governments and how can the Federal Government tax them?
   a. _____
   b. _____

Current Federal Taxes

3. What are the six types of revenue-raising taxes imposed by the Federal Government?
   a. _____
   b. _____
   c. _____
   d. _____
   e. _____
   f. _____

Taxing for Nonrevenue Purposes

4. For what reason other than to raise revenue does Congress levy taxes and how is this power limited?
   a. _____
   b. _____

B. Reviewing Key Terms

5. What is the difference between a progressive tax and a regressive tax? _____
   _____

Place a check mark next to each phrase that correctly pairs a type of tax with an example of that tax.

❒ 6. payroll tax; Medicare

❒ 7. excise tax; federal tax on imported peanuts

❒ 8. progressive tax; income tax

❒ 9. custom duty; tax on tobacco products

❒ 10. regressive tax; Medicare

❒ 11. estate tax; tax on inheritance

❒ 12. tax return; income tax form

❒ 13. gift tax; tax on gifts worth more than $1,000

© Pearson Education, Inc.

Section 2: Guided Reading and Review
Nontax Revenues and Borrowing

CHAPTER
16

A. As You Read

Answer the following questions as you read Section 2.

Nontax Revenues

1. What are sources of interest that the government collects as nontax revenue? _____
_____

2. What is seigniorage? _____
_____

3. What government corporation generates nontax revenue for the government? _____

Borrowing

4. For what three reasons does the government often borrow money? _____
_____
_____

5. Explain the process by which the government borrows money. _____
_____
_____

The Public Debt

6. What has been the trend of the public debt over the past 20 years? _____
_____

B. Reviewing Key Terms

Define the following terms in the space provided.

7. interest _____
_____

8. deficit _____
_____

9. surplus _____
_____

10. public debt _____
_____

Section 3: Guided Reading and Review
Spending and the Budget

A. As You Read

Complete the chart below by filling in the missing information in the blanks provided.

Federal Spending		
Type of Spending	Meaning	Examples
Controllable Spending	1. _____ _____ _____	2. a. _____ b. _____ c. _____
Uncontrollable Spending	3. _____ _____ _____	4. a. _____ b. _____ c. _____

As you read the section, fill in the answers to the questions below.

5. Who initiates the spending process? _____
_____

6. How does the federal budget serve as a political statement? _____
_____

7. According to the chart on page 460, in what three categories has the government spent the
most money since 1997? _____
_____

8. Where does the budget-making process begin? _____
_____

9. How does Congress become involved in the process? _____
_____

10. What happens if the 13 appropriations measures are not passed by the beginning of the fiscal
year? _____
_____

B. Reviewing Key Terms

Explain the meaning of the following term and give some examples.

11. entitlement _____
_____

Section 1: Guided Reading and Review
Foreign Affairs and National Security

A. As You Read

As you read Section 1, answer the questions below in the space provided.

1. What major change took place in the United States' relationship with the rest of the world after World War II? _____
_____

2. What is foreign policy? _____
_____

3. What is the main function of the State Department? _____
_____

4. What does the Foreign Service do? _____
_____

5. Why is the military under civilian control? _____
_____

6. Who are the chief military aides to the secretary of defense? _____
_____

7. What are the three military departments? _____
_____

B. Reviewing Key Terms

Match the descriptions in Column I with the terms in Column II. Write the correct letter in each blank.

Column I

_____ 8. refusal to become involved in the world's affairs

_____ 9. events that take place in one's own country

_____ 10. the right to send and receive diplomatic representatives

_____ 11. freedom of a nation's ambassadors from the laws of the country to which they are accredited

_____ 12. a nation's relationship with other countries

_____ 13. the President's representative to another nation

Column II

a. diplomatic immunity

b. right of legation

c. ambassador

d. isolationism

e. domestic affairs

f. foreign affairs

CHAPTER 17

Section 2: Guided Reading and Review
Other Foreign and Defense Agencies

A. As You Read

Use the following chart to organize information from this section. If an acronym is used, write out the full name of the agency on the blank provided. Then answer the questions below the chart on a separate sheet of paper.

Organization	Function
CIA 1. _____	2. _____ _____ _____
INS 3. _____	4. _____ _____ _____
NASA 5. _____	6. _____ _____ _____
Selective Service System	7. _____ _____

8. What limit has Congress imposed on the operations of the CIA?

9. Briefly describe the history of military conscription in the United States.

B. Reviewing Key Terms

Complete each sentence by writing the correct term in the blank provided.

10. When they reach the age of 18, all men must register for the _____, or compulsory military service.

11. CIA operations include _____, or spying.

12. People suffering persecution in their own countries may come to the United States for _____, or safe haven.

Section 3: Guided Reading and Review
American Foreign Policy Overview

A. As You Read

Using information from Section 3, complete the graphic organizer below.

Key Events in American Foreign Policy		
Dates	**Event**	**Result**
1823	1. _____	The United States stays out of European affairs and warns others to stay out of the Americas.
Early 1900s	2. _____	United States polices Latin America
3._____	Open Door in China	4. _____
5._____	U.S. enters World War I	Intention is "to make world safe for democracy."
1941	Japan bombs United States naval base at Pearl Harbor, Hawaii	6. _____ _____ _____
After World War II	Collective security	7. _____
1947	8. _____	United States supports nations that remain free of Soviet control.
1948–1949	9. _____	After Soviets try to blockade West Berlin, the United States mounts a massive airlift to provide supplies to West Berlin.
1950–1953	10. _____	UN forces, largely American, defend South Korea against Communist North Korea.
11. _____	Cuban Missile Crisis	12. _____
1965–1973	13. _____	United States becomes increasingly involved in a civil war in Vietnam.
14. _____	15. _____	United States and allies deploy troops to force Iraq to withdraw from Kuwait.

B. Reviewing Key Terms

Define the following key terms on a separate sheet of paper.

16. collective security   18. cold war   20. détente

17. deterrence   19. containment

© Pearson Education, Inc.

CHAPTER 17

Section 4: Guided Reading and Review
Foreign Aid and Defense Alliances

A. As You Read

Use the chart below to organize the information presented in the textbook on security alliances.

Name of Pact or Organization	Members	Agreement
NATO	1.	2.
Rio Pact	3.	4.
ANZUS	5.	6.
Japanese Pact	7.	8.
Philippines Pact	9.	10.
Korean Pact	11.	12.

On a separate sheet of paper, describe the duties of each of the United Nations organizations listed below.

13. General Assembly of Justice
14. Security Council
15. Economic and Social Council
16. International Court of Justice
17. Secretariat

B. Reviewing Key Terms

Complete each sentence by writing the correct term in the blank provided.

18. Of all the regions that receive American _____, Asia has received the greatest economic assistance.

19. The Rio Pact is an example of a _____.

20. The nonpermanent members of the _____ are elected to two-year terms by the General Assembly.

Section 1: Guided Reading and Review
The National Judiciary

A. As You Read

As you read Section 1, answer the questions below.

1. What did Article III, Section 1 of the Constitution create? _____
_____

2. What are constitutional courts? _____
_____

3. What are special courts? _____
_____

4. Under what circumstances may federal courts hear a case? _____
_____

5. What is the procedure for the selection of federal judges? _____
_____

6. What is the primary function of federal judges? _____
_____

7. How long are the terms of judges of constitutional courts? _____

8. How long are the terms of judges in special courts? _____

B. Reviewing Key Terms

Write the definition of each term in the left column in the box in the right column.

Term	Definition
exclusive jurisdiction	9.
concurrent jurisdiction	10.
plaintiff	11.
defendant	12.
original jurisdiction	13.
appellate jurisdiction	14.

CHAPTER 18

Section 2: Guided Reading and Review
The Inferior Courts

A. As You Read

As you read Section 2, fill in the chart below to help you organize information about each type of federal court shown.

Court	Number of Courts	Number of Judges	Types of Cases
1. District Court	a.	b.	c.
2. Courts of Appeals	a.	b.	c.
3. Supreme Court	a.	b.	c.
4. Court of International Trade	a.	b.	c.
5. Court of Appeals for the Federal Circuit	a.	b.	c.

Answer the following questions.

6. On what basis is the United States divided into judicial districts? _____

_____

_____

7. When and why were the courts of appeals created? _____

_____

_____

B. Reviewing Key Terms

Define the following terms.

8. criminal case _____

_____

9. civil case _____

_____

10. docket _____

_____

Section 3: Guided Reading and Review

The Supreme Court

A. As You Read

Complete each sentence by finishing it in the blank provided.

1. The term "judicial review" means _____
_____.

2. In the United States, the court of last resort in questions of federal law is _____
_____.

3. The first case in which the court used its power of judicial review was _____
_____.

4. The Supreme Court has original jurisdiction in cases involving _____ or
those affecting _____.

5. A case is accepted if at least _____ Court justices agree to place it on the docket.

6. When the Supreme Court accepts a case, it receives written documents called _____
and hears _____.

7. The opening day of each Supreme Court term is _____.

B. Reviewing Key Terms

Complete each sentence in Column I by writing the letter of the correct term from Column II in the blank.

Column I

_____ 8. A justice who agrees with the Opinion of the Court may nonetheless decide to write a ___.

_____ 9. If the Chief Justice agrees with the Opinion of the Court, he or she decides who will write the ___.

_____ 10. When the Supreme Court accepts a case for review, it issues a ___.

_____ 11. Justices who disagree with an Opinion of the Court may register their views by writing a ___.

_____ 12. If an inferior court wants guidance from the Supreme Court on a particular question of law, it may issue a ___.

Column II

a. writ of certiorari

b. certificate

c. dissenting opinion

d. concurring opinion

e. majority opinion

CHAPTER 18

Section 4: Guided Reading and Review
The Special Courts

A. As You Read

As you read Section 4, fill in the chart below to organize information about each special court shown.

Court	Number of Judges	Term of Judges	Types of Cases
1. United States Court of Federal Claims	a.	b.	c.
2. Territorial Courts			c.
3. Court of Appeals for the Armed Forces	a.	b.	c.
4. Court of Appeals for Veterans Claims	a.	b.	c.
5. United States Tax Court	a.	b.	c.

B. Reviewing Key Terms

Define the following terms.

6. redress _____

_____

7. court-martial _____

_____

8. civilian tribunal _____

_____

© Pearson Education, Inc.

Section 1: Guided Reading and Review
The Unalienable Rights

A. As You Read

Fill in the blanks in the following paragraph with the appropriate words or phrases from the section content.

The Framers believed that the primary purpose of government was to (1.)_____.
They stated this belief both in the (2.) _____ and the (3.) _____.
The Bill of Rights was added to the Constitution because (4.) _____.
This document fit well with the principle of (5.) _____, which states that
governments have only those powers which the people have granted to them. But even in a democracy, individual rights are not unlimited. Each individual's rights are limited by
(6.) _____. Often, the rights of individuals conflict and, when this occurs,
(7.) _____ may be called upon to decide which rights take precedence. For the most
part, the protections of the Bill of Rights are extended to (8.) _____ as well as
(9.) _____, but there are some rights that may be denied to
(10.) _____.

Answer the following question in the space provided.

11. How has the Supreme Court ensured that States do not deny basic rights to the people?

_____

_____

_____

_____

B. Reviewing Key Terms

Match the descriptions in Column I with the terms in Column II. Write the correct letter in each blank.

Column I

_____ **12.** the positive acts of government that seek to make the guarantees of the Constitution a reality for all people

_____ **13.** foreign-born resident; noncitizen

_____ **14.** inclusion of the essential Bill of Rights into the Due Process Clause

_____ **15.** the first 10 amendments to the Constitution, which guarantee certain personal freedoms to all people

_____ **16.** part of the Constitution that prevents States from denying people their basic rights

_____ **17.** protections against government

Column II

a. Bill of Rights
b. civil liberties
c. civil rights
d. alien
e. Due Process Clause
f. process of incorporation

CHAPTER 19

Section 2: Guided Reading and Review
Freedom of Religion

A. As You Read

On a separate sheet of paper, write the decisions for each of the cases listed below. The cases on the left involved an interpretation of the Establishment Clause and the cases on the right involved an interpretation of the Free Exercise Clause.

Establishment Clause
1. *Pierce* v. *Society of Sisters*, 1925
2. *Everson* v. *Board of Education*, 1947
3. *Zorach* v. *Clauson*, 1952
4. *Engel* v. *Vitale*, 1962
5. *Abington School District* v. *Schempp*, 1963
6. *Wallace* v. *Jaffree*, 1985
7. *Santa Fe Independent School District* v. *Doe*, 2000
8. *Lemon* v. *Kurtzman*, 1971
9. *Lynch* v. *Donnelly*, 1984
10. *County of Allegheny* v. *ACLU*, 1989
11. *Marsh* v. *Chambers*, 1983

Free Exercise Clause
12. *Reynolds* v. *United States*, 1879
13. *McGowan* v. *Maryland*, 1961
14. *Welsh* v. *United States*, 1970
15. *Lyng* v. *Northwest Indian Cemetery Protective Association*, 1988
16. *Cantwell* v. *Connecticut*, 1940
17. *Sherbert* v. *Verner*, 1963
18. *West Virginia Board of Education* v. *Barnette*, 1943

B. Reviewing Key Terms

Define the following terms in the space provided.

19. Establishment Clause _____

_____

_____

20. Free Exercise Clause _____

_____

_____

21. parochial _____

_____

_____

Section 3: Guided Reading and Review
Freedom of Speech and Press

A. As You Read

Use the chart to organize information about important Supreme Court rulings in cases involving freedom of speech and press.

Case	Date	Ruling
Schenck v. *United States*	1. _____	2. _____
Miller v. *California*	1973	3. _____
New York Times v. *United States*	4. _____	5. _____
6. _____	7. _____	held that reporters must respond to relevant questions in a valid grand jury investigation or a criminal trial
Burstyn v. *Wilson*	1952	8. _____
9. _____	1940	held that television is protected by the First Amendment, but its protection is very limited
10. _____	1940	struck down a law that made picketing a place of business a crime
Greater New Orleans Broadcasting Association v. *United States*	11. _____	12. _____

B. Reviewing Key Terms

On a separate sheet of paper, define the following terms.

13. libel

14. slander

15. sedition

16. seditious speech

17. prior restraint

18. shield law

19. symbolic speech

20. picketing

Section 4: Guided Reading and Review
Freedom of Assembly and Petition

A. As You Read

The following paragraphs summarize Section 4. As you read the section, fill in the blanks with the missing words or phrases.

The (1.) _____ Amendment guarantees the right of people to (2.) _____, peaceably and to petition government for (3.) _____. The (4.) _____ Amendment extends this protection to actions by State and local governments. However, the Court has allowed government to place reasonable limits on these rights in the form of (5.) _____ regulations. For example, parades cannot be held near a courthouse when court is in session if they are (6.) _____. But government regulation of the right of assembly must be precisely drawn and (7.) _____. In addition, while government can regulate assembly on the basis of (8.) _____, it cannot regulate on the basis of (9.) _____.

Most demonstrations take place in public places because (10.) _____. However, the Court has held that it is permissible for the government to require demonstrators to give (11.) _____ and acquire (12.) _____ before demonstrating in public places.

In the case of *Gregory* v. *Chicago,* 1969, the Court held that demonstrators cannot be charged with disorderly conduct as long as they (13.) _____, even if their actions lead to (14.) _____.

In more recent years, cases have focused on demonstrations at (15.) _____. The Court has held that local ordinances can require a buffer zone to avoid blocking access to them.

Demonstrations on (16.) _____, such as shopping malls, are viewed differently by the Court. The Court has ruled that State supreme courts may interpret State constitutions in such a way as to allow (17.) _____.

B. Reviewing Key Terms

Define the following key terms in the space provided.

18. assemble _____
    _____

19. content neutral _____
    _____

20. guarantee of association _____
    _____

Section 1: Guided Reading and Review
Due Process Law

CHAPTER
20

A. As You Read

Use the chart below to organize information about the legitimate uses of the States' police power.

Uses of the Police Power	
States' Duty to Protect:	**Examples**
Health	1. _____ _____
2. _____ _____	seat-belt laws, drunk driving laws, laws against concealed weapons
Morals	3. _____ _____
4. _____ _____	compulsory education laws, regulation of public utilities, assist medically needy

B. Reviewing Key Terms

Define the following terms on a separate sheet of paper. Then, describe a court case involving each.

5. procedural due process

6. substantive due process

7. right of privacy

In the space provided, use each key term in a sentence that shows the meaning of the term.

8. police power _____

_____

_____

9. search warrant _____

_____

_____

CHAPTER 20

Section 2: Guided Reading and Review
Freedom and Security of the Person

A. As You Read

As you read the section, fill in the chart below. Write the provisions of each amendment in the first column. In the second column, give an example of a Supreme Court ruling that was based on the provisions of each amendment.

Amendment	Provisions	Examples
13th	1.	2.
2nd	3.	4.
3rd	5.	Not Applicable
4th	6.	7.

B. Reviewing Key Terms

Match the descriptions in Column I with the terms in Column II. Write the correct letter in each blank.

Column I

_____ 8. forced labor

_____ 9. a reasonable suspicion of a crime

_____ 10. bias; unfairness

_____ 11. illegally seized evidence cannot be used against the person from whom it was seized

_____ 12. a blanket search warrant

Column II

a. exclusionary rule
b. writ of assistance
c. discrimination
d. probable cause
e. involuntary servitude

Section 3: Guided Reading and Review
Rights of the Accused

A. As You Read

Copy the chart below onto a separate sheet of paper and then fill in the blanks to organize information about the legal terms introduced in this section.

Legal Term	Definition	Purpose
writ of habeas corpus	1.	2.
bill of attainder	3.	4.
5.	criminal law that applies to an act committed before its passage	6.
indictment	7.	prevents overzealous prosecutors from recklessly charging people with crimes
8.	formal accusation brought by a grand jury on its own motion	allows grand jury to act when a prosecutor has some interest in not prosecuting
double jeopardy	9.	10.
bench trial	11.	the defendant always has the right to a jury trial, but that may be waived if the defendant is fully aware of his or her rights
12.	13.	to prevent the police from coercing confessions or self-incriminating testimony from uninformed suspects

Answer the following questions on a separate sheet of paper.

14. What four criteria are used to determine if a trial delay is unconstitutional?

15. What is a petit jury?

16. What was the Supreme Court's ruling in *Escobedo* v. *Illinois,* 1964?

17. What does the 5th Amendment ban?

B. Reviewing Key Terms

Define the following term on a separate sheet of paper.

18. grand jury

CHAPTER 20

Section 4: Guided Reading and Review
Punishment

A. As You Read

Each of the statements under the main heading in the outline below is incorrect. Rewrite each on a separate sheet of paper to make it correct.

Bail and Preventive Detention

1. Every person accused of a crime must be allowed to set his or her own bail.

2. The Supreme Court rejected preventive detention in *Stack* v. *Boyle*, 1951.

Cruel and Unusual Punishment

3. The 6th Amendment prohibits cruel and unusual punishment and the 13th Amendment extends that prohibition to the States.

4. The Supreme Court has ruled that death by firing squad is cruel and unusual.

Capital Punishment

5. Thirty States have capital punishment laws.

6. A State can impose the death penalty only for crimes resulting in excessive cruelty to the victim.

Treason

7. Treason is the only crime specifically defined in the Constitution because the Framers knew that its meaning would be lost with time.

8. A person can be convicted of treason if there is one eyewitness to the treasonous act.

B. Reviewing Key Terms

Match the descriptions in Column I with the terms in Column II. Write the correct letter in each blank.

Column I

_____ 9. levying war against the United States or giving aid and comfort to its enemies

_____ 10. holding the accused without bail when there is reason to believe the accused will commit serious crimes before trial

_____ 11. money an accused person must deposit with the court to guarantee an appearance at trial

_____ 12. the death penalty

Column II

a. bail

b. preventive detention

c. capital punishment

d. treason

Section 1: Guided Reading and Review

CHAPTER
21

Diversity and Discrimination in American Society

A. As You Read

As you read the section, summarize the information given on each group below in the space provided.

African Americans	Native Americans	Hispanic Americans
1. _____ _____ _____ _____	2. _____ _____ _____ _____	3. _____ _____ _____ _____

Asian Americans	Women
4. _____ _____ _____ _____ _____	5. _____ _____ _____ _____ _____

B. Reviewing Key Terms

Place a check mark next to each of the following pairs that correctly matches a term from this chapter with its definition.

❑   6. reservation—land set aside by the government for Native-American use

❑   7. heterogeneous—made up of several ingredients

❑   8. assimilation—agreement

❑   9. refugee—person who comes to the United States for religious reasons

❑ 10. immigrant—new citizen

Section 2: Guided Reading and Review
Equality Before the Law

A. As You Read

Complete the outline by supplying the missing words or phrases in the blanks.

Equal Protection Clause

1. Reasonable Classification—The government is allowed to _____, or draw distinctions, between groups, but it may not do so _____.

2. The Rational Basis Test—The rational basis test asks: Does the classification in question bear a reasonable relationship to the achievement of some _____ _____?

3. The Strict Scrutiny Test—In cases dealing with "_____," such as the right to vote, or "_____," such as those based on race or sex, the Supreme Court imposes the strict scrutiny test, which requires that the State prove that some "_____" justifies the distinctions it has drawn.

Segregation in America

4. The Separate-but-Equal Doctrine—In 1896, the Supreme Court upheld racial segregation by saying that segregated facilities for African Americans were lawful as long as the separate facilities were _____.

5. *Brown* v. *Topeka Board of Education,* 1954—In 1954 the Court reversed itself, ruling that segregation was _____ and must be ended.

6. De Jure and De Facto Segregation—Attention turned toward schools that practiced _____, often brought about by housing patterns.

Classification by Sex

7. Until 20 years ago, the Court has upheld _____ classifications.

8. Today, sex is a "suspect classification," and is allowed only in cases where the law is intended to serve an "important _____ objective."

B. Reviewing Key Terms

Define the following terms on a separate sheet of paper.

9. segregation

10. Jim Crow law

11. separate-but-equal doctrine

12. integration

13. de jure segregation

14. de facto segregation

Guided Reading and Review

Section 3: Guided Reading and Review
Federal Civil Rights Laws

A. As You Read

Use the time line to organize information on the legislation and Supreme Court cases dealing with civil rights. Fill in the appropriate act or case for each date indicated on the time line in the space provided. Then explain the significance of each event.

Federal Civil Rights Laws

2.		4.		7., 8.		9.	
1960	1968	1979		1989		1995	2000

	1964	1970	1978	1980	1987	1990	1996
	1.		3.	5.	6.		10.

1. _____

2. _____

3. _____

4. _____

5. _____

6. _____

7. _____

8. _____

9. _____

10. _____

B. Reviewing Key Terms

Define the following terms on a separate sheet of paper.

11. affirmative action

12. quota

13. reverse discrimination

CHAPTER 21 Section 4: Guided Reading and Review
American Citizenship

A. As You Read

Use the information from Section 4 to complete the chart below.

Changes in U.S. Immigration Policy		
Date	Policy	Features
Independence– 1880s	Open frontier	1._____
1882	2. _____	severely limited immigration from Asia
1921–1929	Immigration Acts of 1921, 1924, and the National Origins Act of 1929	3._____ _____
4._____	5. _____ _____	modified quotas to cover all countries outside Western Hemisphere
1965	Immigration Act of 1965	6._____ _____
7._____	Immigration Act of 1990	8._____ _____

Answer the following question on a separate sheet of paper.

9. Write a paragraph summarizing the information provided under the heading "Undocumented Aliens."

B. Reviewing Key Terms

Match the descriptions in Column I with the terms in Column II. Write the correct letter in each blank.

Column I

_____ 10. citizen of a foreign state living in this country

_____ 11. legal process by which a person becomes a citizen of a country at some time after birth

_____ 12. one who owes allegiance to the state and is entitled to its protection

_____ 13. legal process by which citizenship is lost

_____ 14. involuntary loss of citizenship by someone not born here, usually because of fraud

_____ 15. legally requiring an alien to leave the United States

_____ 16. the law of the soil; where one is born

_____ 17. the law of the blood; to whom one is born

Column II

a. citizen

b. jus soli

c. jus sanguinis

d. naturalization

e. alien

f. expatriation

g. denaturalization

h. deportation

© Pearson Education, Inc.

Section 1: Guided Reading and Review
Great Britain

A. As You Read

The chart below compares the governments of the United States and Great Britain. As you read Section 1, complete the chart by filling in the information that describes the government of Great Britain for each category shown.

A Comparison of the Governments of the United States and Great Britain		
	United States	Great Britain
Constitution	Written	1.
Monarch	None	2.
Government Powers	Separated	3.
Legislative Body	Bicameral Congress (Senate; House of Representatives)	4.
Executive	President (head of state and head of government)	5.
Elections	Regularly scheduled (representatives, 2 years; senators, 6 years; President, 4 years)	6.
Parties	2 major parties (Republican and Democratic)	7.
National and Local Government	Separate federal and State governments	8.
Judiciary	Independent Supreme Court	9.

B. Reviewing Key Terms

Define the following terms on a separate sheet of paper.

10. monarchy
11. by-election
12. coalition
13. minister
14. shadow cabinet
15. devolution

© Pearson Education, Inc.

CHAPTER
22

Section 2: Guided Reading and Review
Japan

A. As You Read

As you read Section 2, answer the following questions on a separate sheet of paper.

1. What type of government did Japan have until the 1850s–1860s?

2. What was Japan's objective after it encountered Western powers?

3. What event caused a dramatic change in Japanese politics from 1945 to 1952?

4. What form of government did Americans force the Japanese to accept?

5. What unique feature did the new constitution have?

6. What is the House of Councillors and what kind of power does it have?

7. What is the House of Representatives and what kind of power does it have?

8. What is political consensus and what role does it play in Japanese politics?

9. What causes the prime minister and the cabinet to maintain agreement on most issues?

10. What is the bureaucracy and what role does it play in Japanese government?

11. Which party dominated Japanese politics during most of the period after World War II?

12. How are Japanese courts like the courts of the United States?

B. Reviewing Key Terms

Complete each sentence in Column I by writing the letter of the correct term from Column II in the blank.

Column I

_____ 13. For political purposes, Japan has been divided into 47 districts called ___.

_____ 14. The prime minister has the power to dissolve the House of Representatives, a step called ___, which leads to immediate elections.

_____ 15. The ___ is the name of the Japanese parliament.

_____ 16. An area that has more than one representative is known as a ___.

_____ 17. The Japanese value ___, or broad agreement on political issues.

Column II

a. National Diet

b. prefectures

c. multiseat district

d. consensus

e. dissolution

NAME _____ CLASS _____ DATE _____

A. As You Read

As you read Section 3, complete the chart below comparing the government of Mexico to that of the United States. Then answer the question that follows on a separate sheet of paper.

	Mexico	United States
Early History	Gained independence from 1. _____	Gained independence from England
Three Branches of Government	2. _____ 3. _____ 4. _____	Executive, Legislative, Judicial
Presidential Term	May serve 5. _____ 6. _____-year term(s)	May serve two four-year terms
Congress	Bicameral: 7. _____ and 8. _____	Bicameral: Senate and House of Representatives
Court System	9. _____ _____	Independent system of State and federal courts
Political Parties	10. _____ 11. _____ 12. _____	Two major parties: Democratic and Republican

13. What major change took place with the election of President Vicente Fox in 2000?

B. Reviewing Key Terms

Complete each sentence by writing the correct term in the blank provided.

14. Since 1938 the _____ of the oil industry has served as a symbol of Mexican independence from foreign domination.

15. Mexico has a _____ culture, made up of both Spanish and Native American elements.

16. The free-trade agreement known as _____ removes trade restrictions among the United States, Mexico, and Canada.

© Pearson Education, Inc.

CHAPTER
22

Section 4: Guided Reading and Review
Russia

A. As You Read

The incomplete chronological chart below outlines some of the dramatic events of Russian and Soviet political history. As you read Section 4, fill in the missing event.

Major Russian Political Events	
Year	Event
1721	1.
1905	2.
1917	3.
1924	4.
1950s–1990s	5.
1985	6.
1991	7.
1993	8.
1999	9.

Answer the following questions on a separate sheet of paper.

10. What is the structure of Russia's legislature?

11. What kinds of local governments are there in the Russian Federation?

B. Reviewing Key Terms

Define the following terms in the space provided.

12. purge _____

_____

13. soviet _____

_____

14. *perestroika* _____

_____

15. *glasnost* _____

_____

Section 5: Guided Reading and Review

China

A. As You Read

Using information from Section 5, complete the chart below, which shows the organization of the Chinese Communist party.

Unit	Role
National Party Congress	1. _____ _____
2. _____	elects the Politburo
Politburo	3. _____ _____
4. _____	makes day-to-day decisions for the party (and therefore the government)

On a separate sheet of paper, answer the following questions as you read Section 5.

5. When did China's present form of government begin and who was its leader?

6. How have China's constitutions been different from the constitutions of the United States and most other countries?

7. What organization effectively controls China's government?

8. What are the two main parts of China's national government?

9. What is the structure of China's judicial system?

10. How is Hong Kong governed?

B. Reviewing Key Terms

Complete each sentence by writing the correct term in the blank provided.

11. In 1966, during the _____, the Red Guards attacked teachers, intellectuals, and others who did not have sufficient revolutionary enthusiasm.

12. China includes five_____, or independent, regions.

© Pearson Education, Inc.

Section 1: Guided Reading and Review
Capitalism

A. As You Read

On a separate sheet of paper, copy and complete the chart by writing answers to the questions in the space provided.

1. What are the four factors of production?

   a. _____

   b. _____

   c. _____

   d. _____

2. What are four characteristics of a free enterprise system?

   a. _____

   b. _____

   c. _____

   d. _____

Capitalism

3. Describe the laws of supply and demand.

   _____

   _____

   _____

4. What are three kinds of businesses and what are their advantages and disadvantages?

   a. _____

   b. _____

   c. _____

B. Reviewing Key Terms

Answer the following questions in the space provided.

5. What is the difference between a capitalist and an entrepreneur? _____

   _____

   _____

6. Describe the laissez-faire theory. _____

   _____

   _____

A. As You Read

The main points of Section 2 are supplied in the outline below. As you read the section, fill in the supporting points in the form of answers to the questions.

Socialism

1. What is socialism? _____

_____

The Industrial Revolution

2. What was the Industrial Revolution? _____

_____

3. Who was Karl Marx? _____

_____

4. What did Marx think of capitalism? _____

_____

5. How were socialism and communism alike and different? _____

_____

Characteristics of Socialist Economies

6. What is nationalization? _____

_____

7. How did socialists hope to help the masses? _____

_____

8. Why is taxation high in socialist countries? _____

_____

9. Describe the term "command economy." _____

_____

Socialism in Developing Countries

10. What attracts developing countries to socialism? _____

_____

Pros and Cons

11. What are three major criticisms of socialism? _____

_____

B. Reviewing Key Terms

Define the following terms on a separate sheet of paper.

12. proletariat   14. welfare state   16. centrally planned economy

13. bourgeoisie   15. market economy

CHAPTER 23

Section 3: Guided Reading and Review
Communism

A. As You Read

The chart below lists four concepts Marx analyzed as they related to capitalism. As you read Section 3, complete the chart by explaining Marx's view of each concept.

Marx's Views on Capitalism	
View of history	1.
Value theory	2.
Nature of the state	3.
Dictatorship of the proletariat	4.

List the four main characteristics of communist economies.

5. _____

6. _____

7. _____

8. _____

B. Reviewing Key Terms

Define the following key terms in the space provided.

9. communism _____
_____

10. Gosplan _____
_____

11. privatization _____
_____

12. Great Leap Forward _____
_____

13. commune _____
_____

NAME _____ CLASS _____ DATE _____

A. As You Read

As you read Section 1, write the answers to the questions in the space provided.

Describe the five main categories by which all State constitutions can be described.

1. _____
2. _____
3. _____
4. _____
5. _____

Fill in the chart to explain the amendment process for State constitutions.

Amendments can be proposed by:	Amendments can be ratified by:
6. _____	9. _____
7. _____	
8. _____	

10. Explain the difference between statutory law and fundamental law. _____
_____
_____
_____

B. Reviewing Key Terms

Explain each of the following key terms in the space provided.

11. popular sovereignty _____
_____

12. limited government _____
_____

13. initiative _____
_____

© Pearson Education, Inc.

CHAPTER 24

Section 2: Guided Reading and Review
State Legislatures

A. As You Read

As you read Section 2, write the answers to the questions on the lines provided.

1. What formal qualifications do most States set out for membership in the legislature? _____
_____
_____

2. What is the usual term for State legislators? _____
_____
_____

3. What are eight of the most important legislative powers of State legislatures? _____
_____
_____

4. Name three nonlegislative functions of State legislatures. _____
_____
_____

5. How does the committee system in State legislatures work? _____
_____
_____

6. From where do a large number of bills originate? _____
_____
_____

B. Reviewing Key Terms

Define the following terms on the lines provided.

7. constituent power _____
_____

8. police power _____
_____

9. referendum _____
_____

Section 3: Guided Reading and Review
The Governor and State Administration

A. As You Read

As you read Section 3, complete the chart with information about the governor's powers.

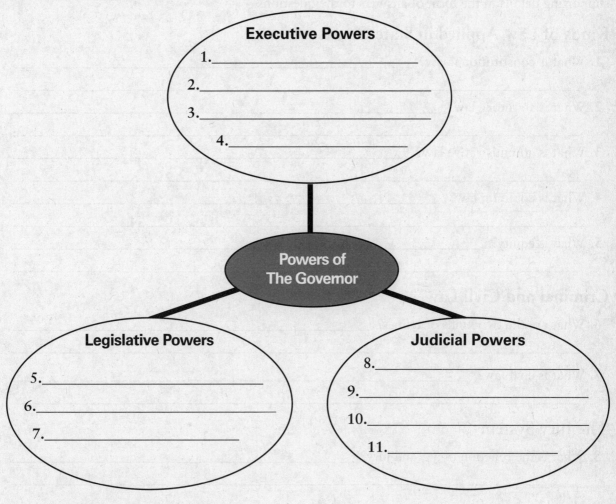

Executive Powers

1._____

2._____

3._____

4._____

Powers of The Governor

Legislative Powers

5._____

6._____

7._____

Judicial Powers

8._____

9._____

10._____

11._____

B. Reviewing Key Terms

Complete each sentence by writing the correct term in the blank provided.

12. The governor has the power to _____, or postpone, the execution of a sentence.

13. The governor has the power to _____, or release a person from the legal consequences of a crime.

14. The governor has the power to _____, or release a prisoner short of the completion of the term of his or her sentence.

15. The governor has the power of _____, or reducing a sentence.

CHAPTER 24

Section 4: Guided Reading and Review
In the Courtroom

A. As You Read

The main points of Section 4 are supplied in the outline. As you read the section, fill in the supporting details in the form of answers to the questions.

Kinds of Law Applied in State Courts

1. What is constitutional law? _____

_____

2. What is statutory law? _____

_____

3. What is administrative law? _____

_____

4. What is common law? _____

_____

5. What is equity? _____

_____

Criminal and Civil Law

6. What are the two kinds of crimes? _____

_____

7. What is civil law? _____

_____

The Jury System

8. What is the function of a grand jury? _____

_____

9. How has the makeup of petit juries changed over the years? _____

_____

10. How are members of a petit jury chosen? _____

_____

B. Reviewing Key Terms

Answer the following question on a separate sheet of paper.

11. What is a precedent and what part do precedents play in common law?

Section 5: Guided Reading and Review
The Courts and Their Judges

A. As You Read

The chart below shows the various types of State and local courts. Next to the name of each type of State and local court, briefly describe the kind of cases heard by that court.

State and Local Courts	
Justice of the Peace	1.
Magistrate's Court	2.
Municipal Court	3.
Juvenile Court	4.
General Trial Court	5.
Intermediate Appellate Court	6.
State Supreme Court	7.

B. Reviewing Key Terms

Use each key term below in a sentence that shows the meaning of the term.

8. warrant _____

_____

9. preliminary hearing _____

10. appellate jurisdiction _____

_____

Section 1: Guided Reading and Review
Counties, Towns, and Townships

A. As You Read

The outline below lists the main points of Section 1. As you read the section, fill in the supporting details by answering the questions on a separate sheet of paper.

The Counties

1. What are some statistics about the extremes of county sizes and populations?

2. What powers does the typical county government have?

3. What are some of the titles of elected county officials and what do they do?

4. How many people work in county government bureaucracies throughout the United States?

Functions of Counties

5. What are some major functions performed by county governments?

Towns and Townships

6. What is unique about the New England town?

7. How do townships in New York, New Jersey, and Pennsylvania differ from those in Ohio and westward?

Special Districts

8. What are some jobs undertaken by special districts?

B. Reviewing Key Terms

Complete each sentence by writing the correct term in the blank provided.

9. In Alaska, the main unit of local government is the _____.

10. In most of the United States, including Texas, the main unit of local government is the _____.

11. A(n) _____ is an independent unit of local government set up to handle a specific problem or task.

12. In Louisiana, the main unit of local government is the _____.

13. In the Midwest, counties are usually divided into subunits known as _____, which share the duties of local government.

Section 2: Guided Reading and Review
Cities and Metropolitan Areas

CHAPTER
25

A. As You Read

As you read Section 2, fill in the chart below with information about the three forms of city government.

Forms of City Government	Description
Mayor Council Form	1.
Strong mayor	2.
Weak mayor	3.
Commission Form	4.
Council Manager Form	5.

Answer the following questions in the space provided.

6. What is the practice of zoning and why is it important to city planning? _____

_____

7. Briefly describe the reasons for suburban growth. _____

_____

B. Reviewing Key Terms

Define the following key terms in the space provided.

8. incorporation _____

_____

9. charter _____

_____

10. metropolitan area _____

_____

CHAPTER 25

Section 3: Guided Reading and Review
Providing Important Services

A. As You Read

As you read Section 3, complete the chart by writing examples of each of the State-provided services shown.

State Services	Example
Education	
Higher education	1.
Primary and secondary education	2.
Public Welfare	
Health	3.
Welfare	4.
Public Safety	5.
Highways	6.
Other Services	7.

B. Reviewing Key Terms

Fill in the missing terms to complete the following sentences.

8. The Aid to Families with Dependent Children (AFDC) is a(n) _____ program, meaning that anyone meeting eligibility requirements can receive benefits.

9. States help out citizens through _____, or cash assistance for the poor.

10. Low income families can get medical insurance through _____.

11. State budgets depend on the population sizes of its cities and suburbs or its level of _____.

Section 4: Guided Reading and Review
Financing State and Local Government

CHAPTER
25

A. As You Read

As you read Section 4, complete the diagram by writing the various sources of State and local revenues in the space provided.

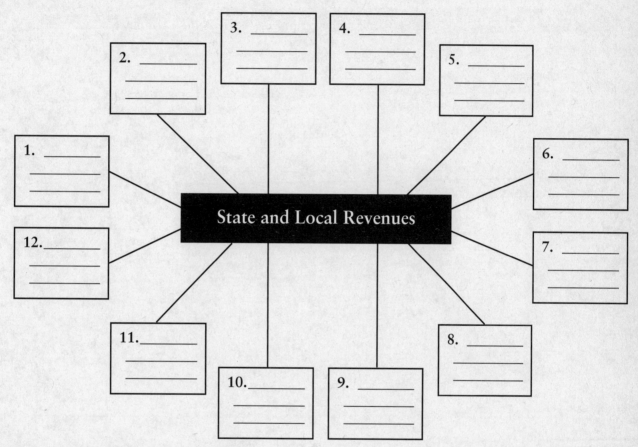

State and Local Revenues

1. _____
2. _____
3. _____
4. _____
5. _____
6. _____
7. _____
8. _____
9. _____
10. _____
11. _____
12. _____

B. Reviewing Key Terms

Read each statement below. If a statement is true, write T in the blank provided. If it is false, write F.

_____ 13. A sales tax is one that is placed on the sale of commodities such as gasoline and cigarettes.

_____ 14. The assessed value of taxable property is always determined on a fair and equal basis.

_____ 15. Inheritance and estate taxes are also known as "death taxes" because they are levied after a person dies.

_____ 16. The sales tax is probably the most difficult tax for a State to collect.

_____ 17. Taxes that are geared according to a person's ability to pay are called regressive taxes.

_____ 18. Generally, taxes placed on the annual income of individuals and corporations are progressive.

CURRICULUM